hOw tO dRaW aNd pAiNt aMeLiA

bY aMy wAtSoN

chipmunkapublishing
the mental health publisher

Amy Watson

All rights reserved, no part of this publication may be reproduced by any means, electronic, mechanical photocopying, documentary, film or in any other format without prior written permission of the publisher.

Published by
Chipmunkapublishing
United Kingdom

http://www.chipmunkapublishing.com

Copyright © Amy Watson 2017

ISBN 978-1-78382-299-7

About Chipmunkapublishing

Mental health books give a voice to writers with mental illness around the world. At Chipmunkapublishing we raise awareness of mental health and the stigma surrounding mental health problems by encouraging society to listen. We are documenting mental health literature as a genre so history does not forget the survivors and carers of people with mental illness and disabilities.

My book is a self-help book about how to draw and paint. It was done over a period of time in a studio. I go into detail about the date and time, what might have happened on that day, what I did in the studio, and what I drew.

Amy Watson

For Elliot

How To Draw and Paint Amelia

Amy Watson

2/12/16, 5:00 p.m.
1. I drew the left side of the face-the ear, hair, the mermaid's left arm. I loved drawing the first line. I made my mark. I had to make the ear bigger.

How To Draw and Paint Amelia

2/13/16, 10:15 p.m.
2. I drew the curve of the chin and it felt great though I felt controlled. I created shapes for shading the ear. I did a lot of erasing near the left side of the forehead for flowers.

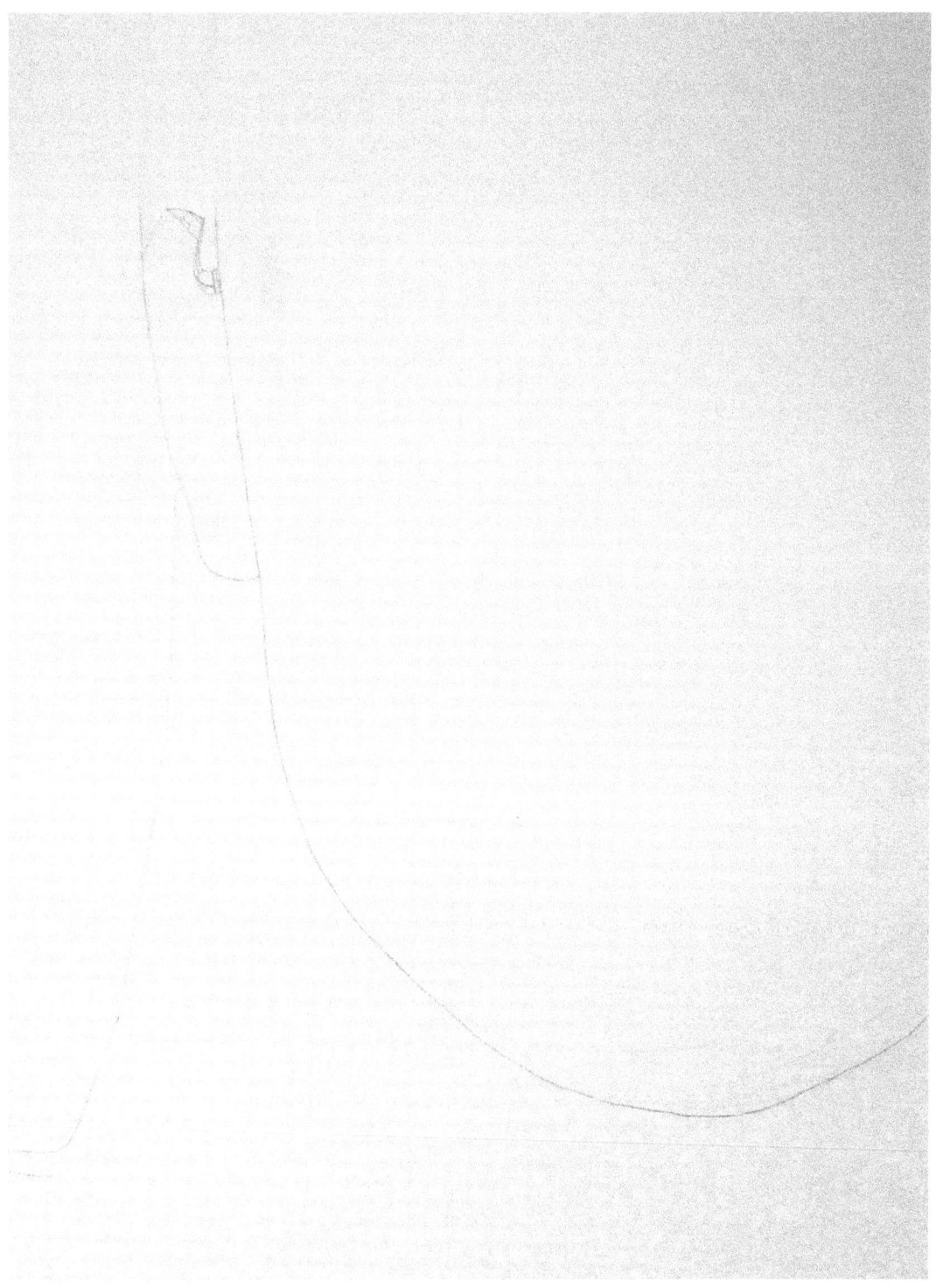

Amy Watson

2/15/16, 5:35 p.m.
3. I spent the whole time on the ear, since this morning while drinking a lot of coffee and tea. I take my time and pretend it's a little city-busy with a lot of detail to make it interesting. I made the opening of the ear too big.

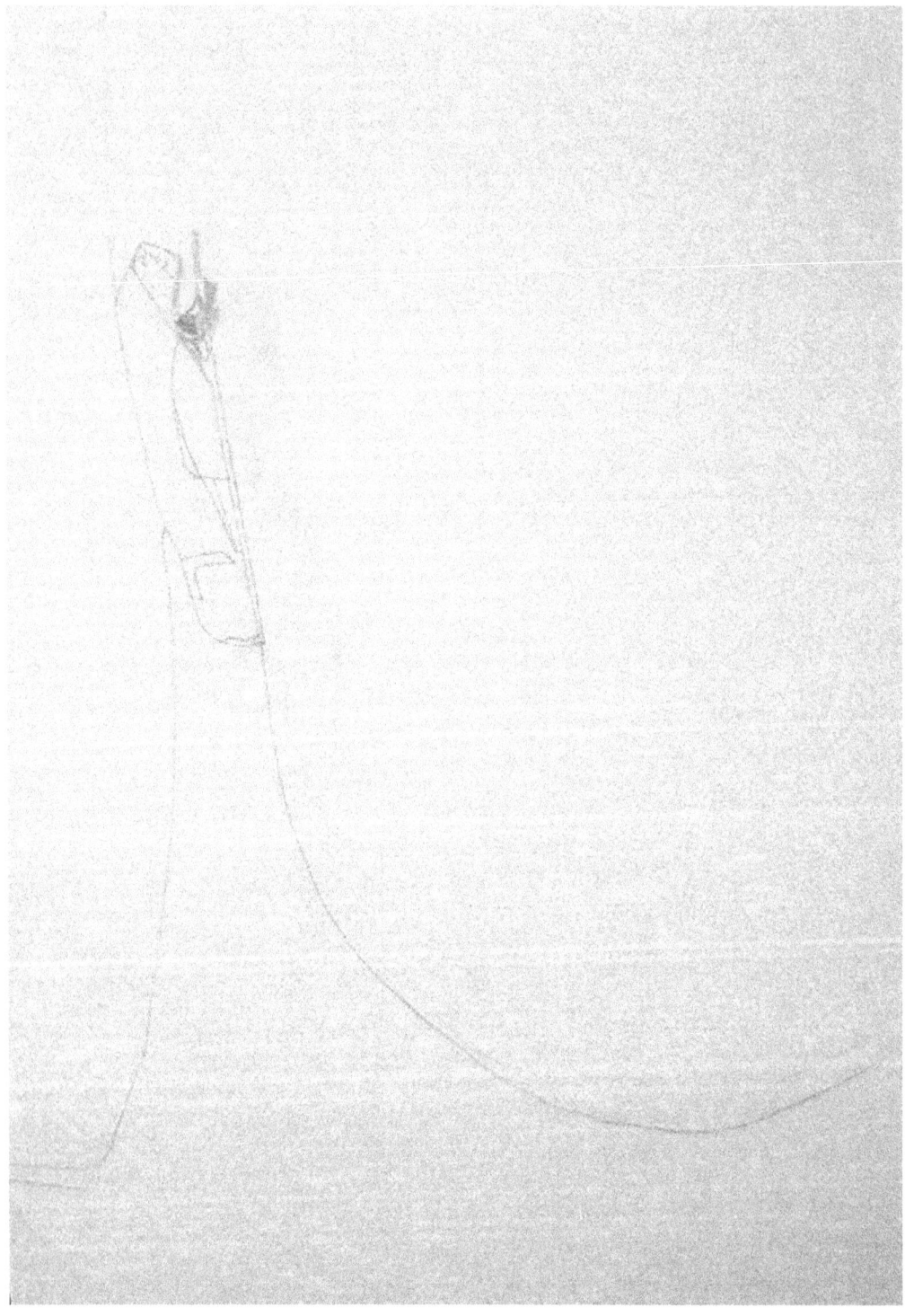

How To Draw and Paint Amelia

2/16/16, 9:15 p.m.
4. Got here late, because my boyfriend had to plow, so I was unmotivated. Finished ear. Want to add a lot of detail so it doesn't look like a big rushed picture. I have all the time in the world and don't want to be interrupted. Looking forward to the next spot.

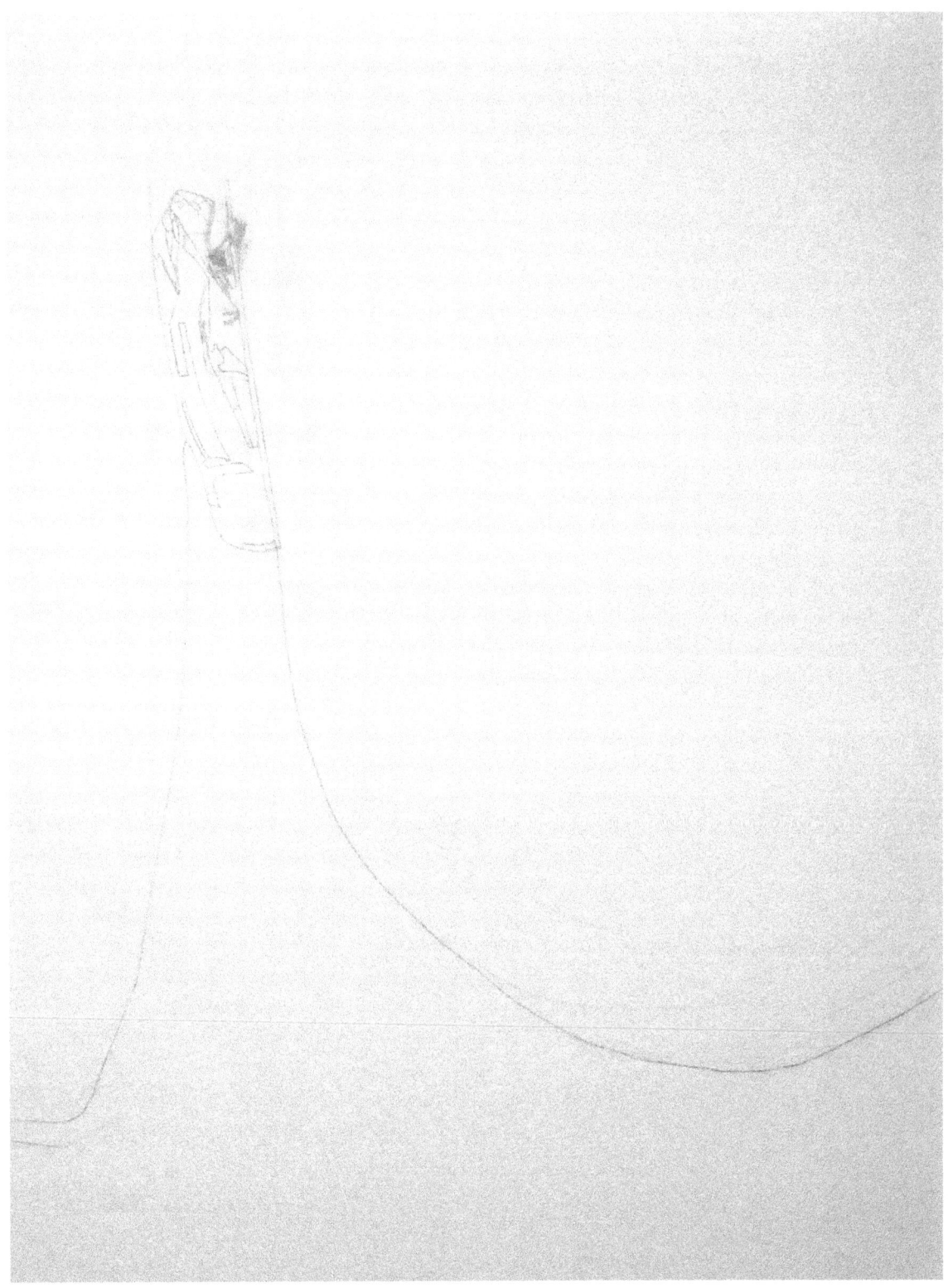

Amy Watson

2/17/16, 9:05 p.m.
  5. Finished up the ear. Completed a flower and moved on to a second one. Looking beautiful. Came here a little late again today so stayed later. I will come in the late morning tomorrow. I need more pencils.

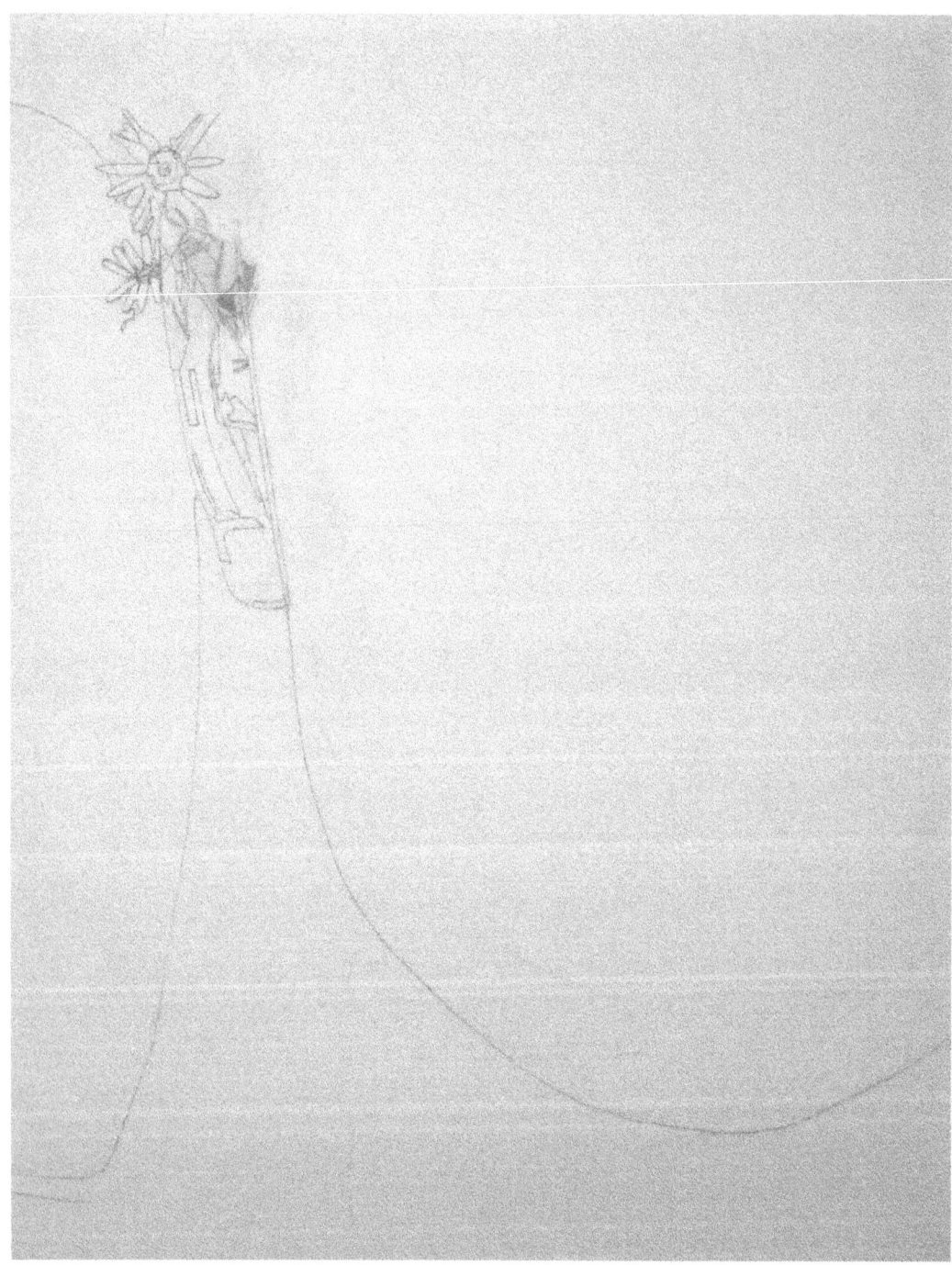

2/18/16, 6:55 p.m.
6. Thinking a lot about mysteries. Must be because I called my friend. Finished second flower, but need to create stem. A lot of intricate lines and dots in the center.

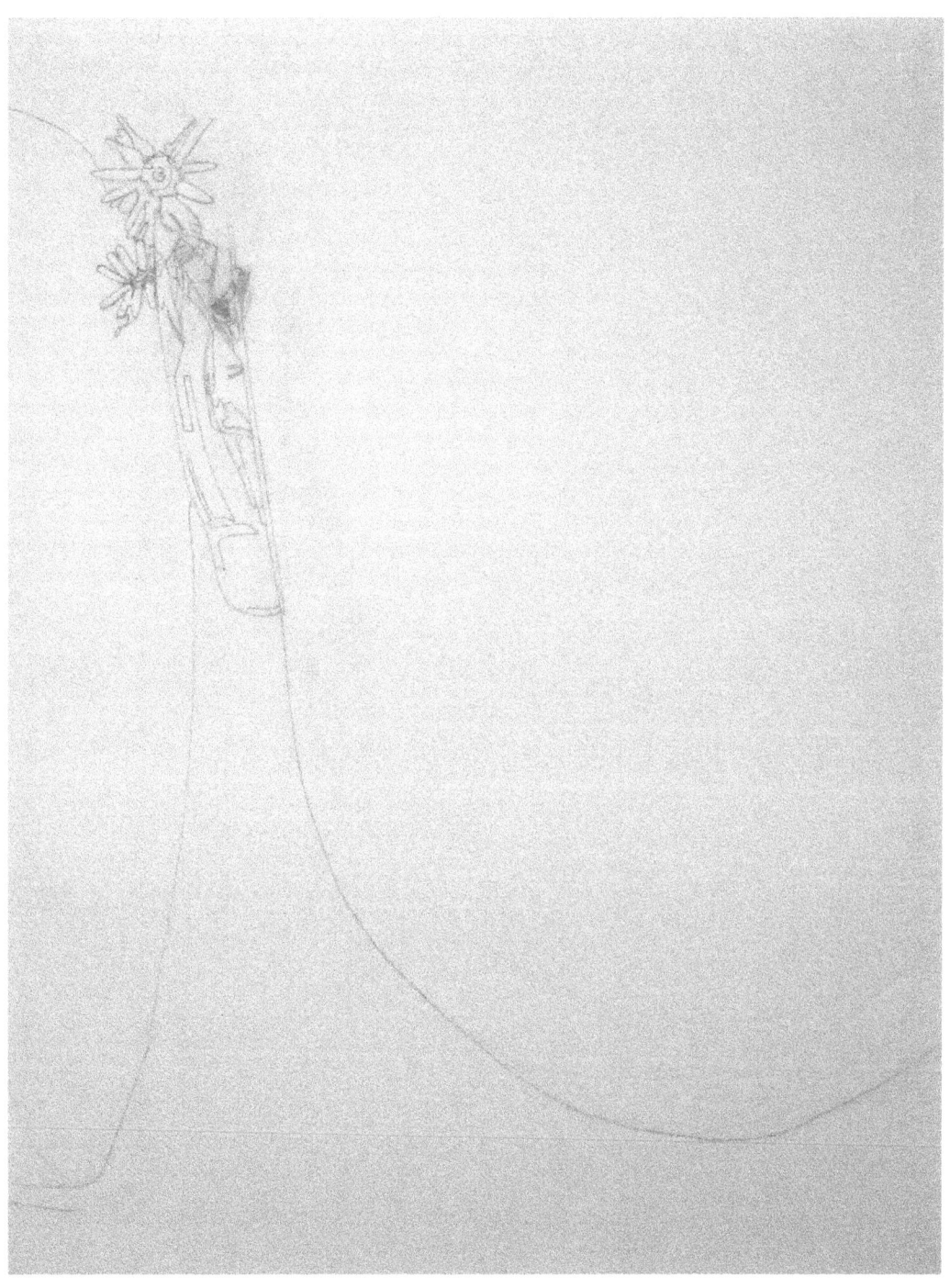

Amy Watson

2/19/16, 9:05 p.m.
7. Got here late. Card wouldn't work. Waiting for replacement. Ate vegetables. Bought pencils. Realized second flower was way too small, but is hidden behind ear, so it looks practical. Finished leaves which are too small. Started next flower.

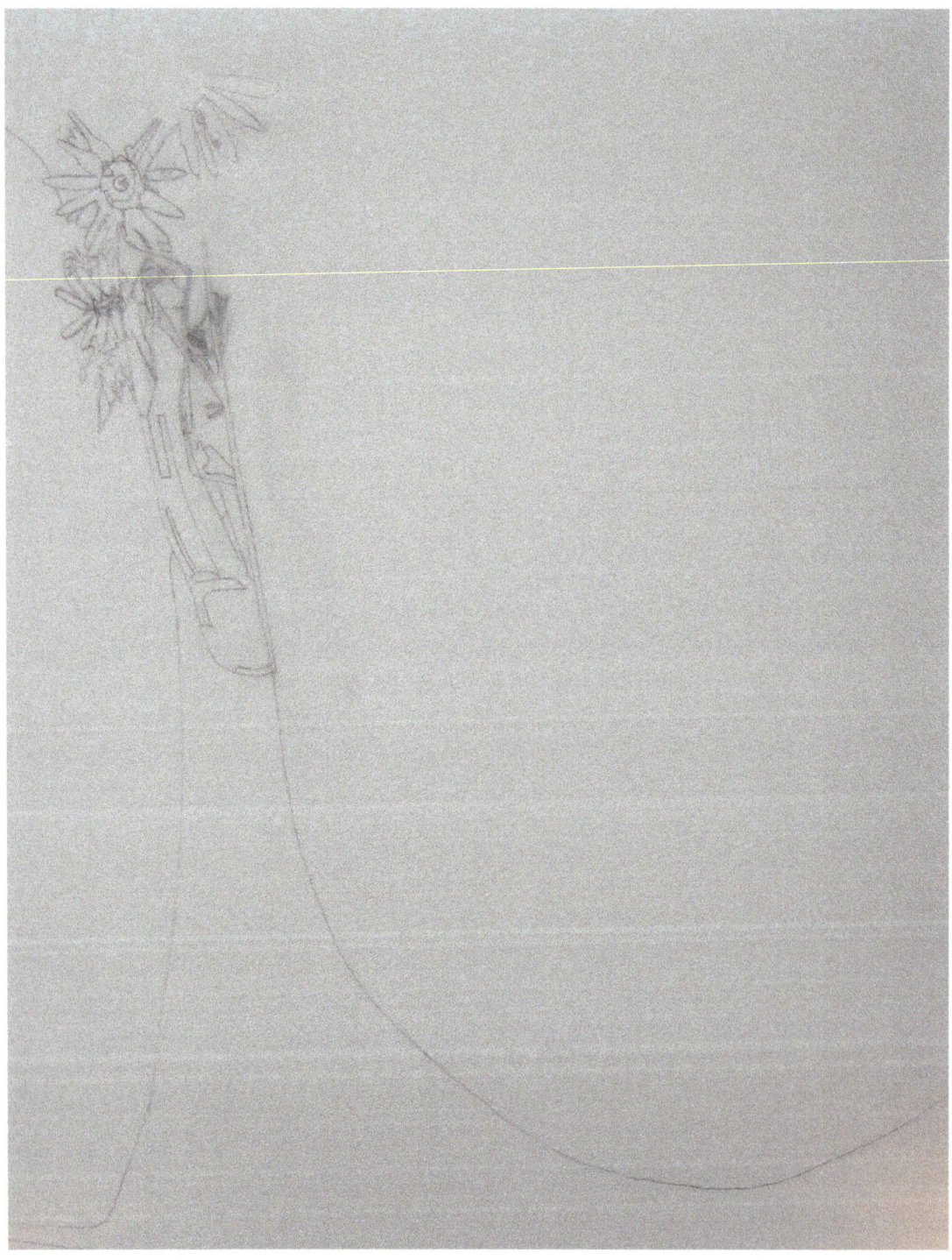

2/20/16, 2:15 p.m.
8. Continued with second flower. Walked. Came because my boyfriend complained about roast beef-not eating it. Candles are making me sick. Will go to Mom's to have shrimp scampi and beep stew.

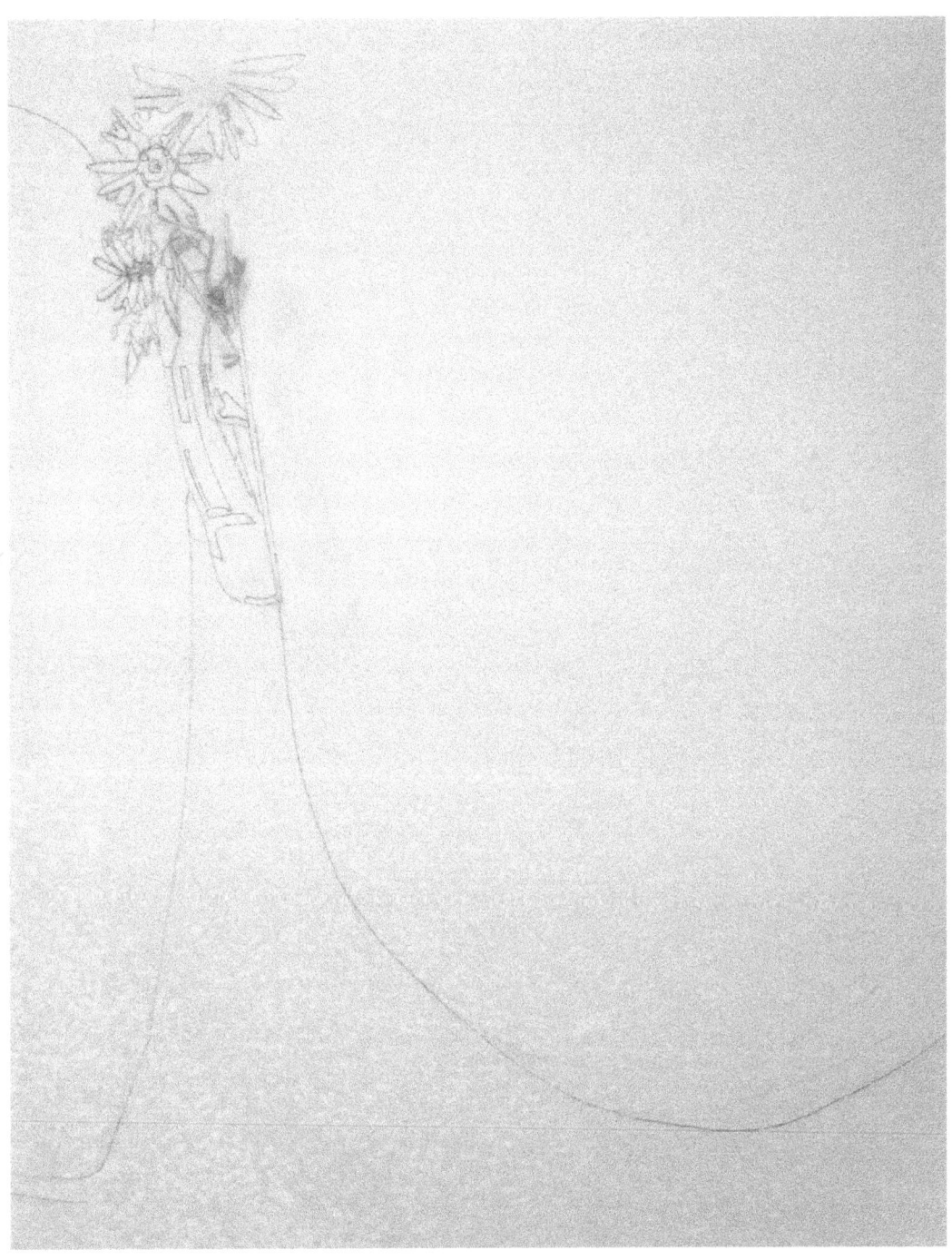

Amy Watson

2/22/16, 6:05 p.m.
9. The second flower is just about finished then onto the leaves. Hopefully everything will be easier. Takes time. Music helps. Seems more structured today, but working hard. My boyfriend was yelling, so came early.

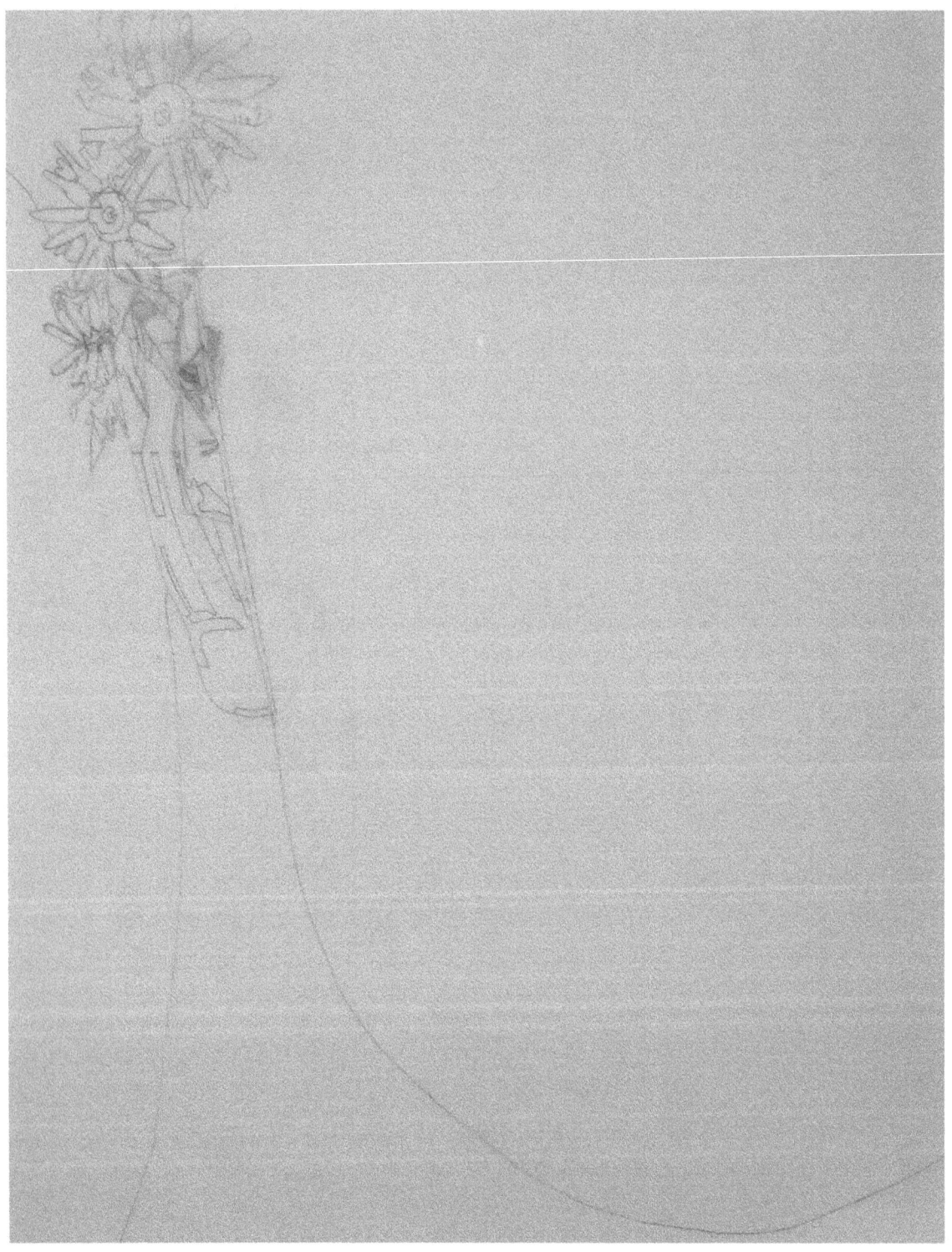

2/23/16, 8:45 p.m.
10. Finished last flower detail. Started leaves. Started background on the left. Hopefully the rest will be smooth sailing. Brought votive candles and used a mixture of wines which weren't as strong.

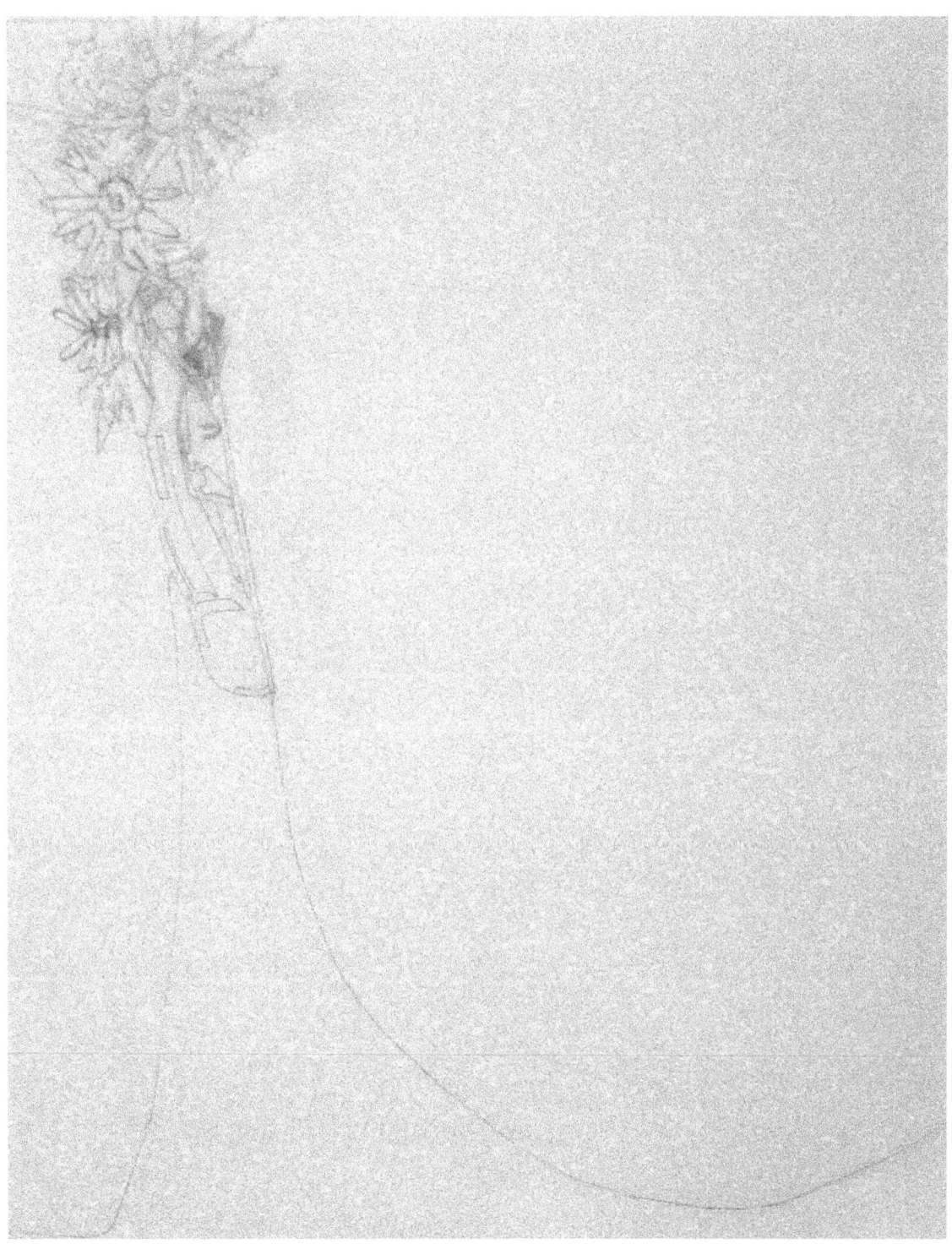

Amy Watson

2/24/16, 8:00 p.m.
11. Got to a late start. Continued with the limbs. Went through make-up. Received a call to leave early to pick up pellets and grocery shop. Set up fountain on magic box when entered.

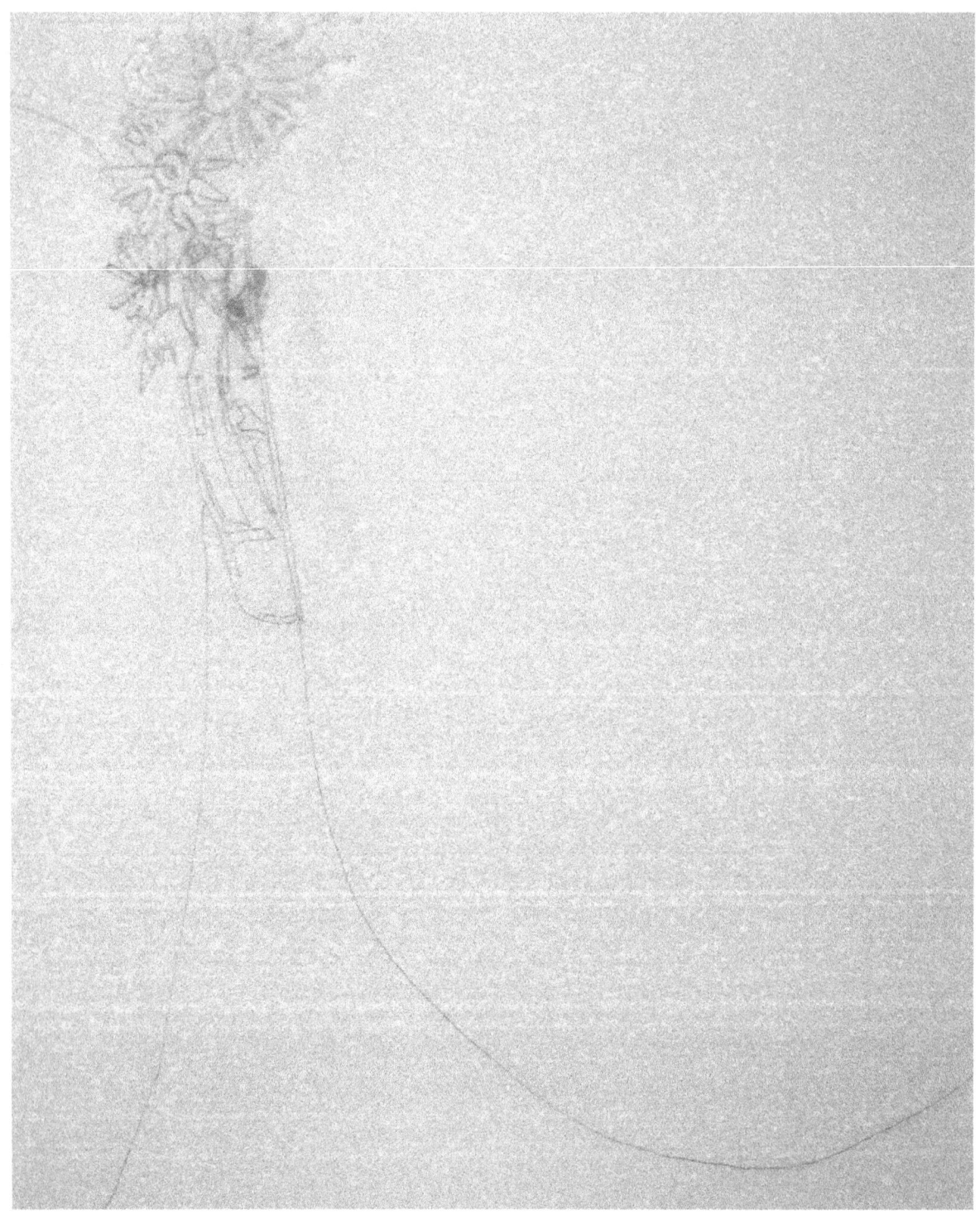

2/25/16, 4:50 p.m.
12. Didn't get much done today, because I took pictures to mix things up and post something to show. I finished the leaves. I drew a line for the bangs. I'm happy I will continue with that.

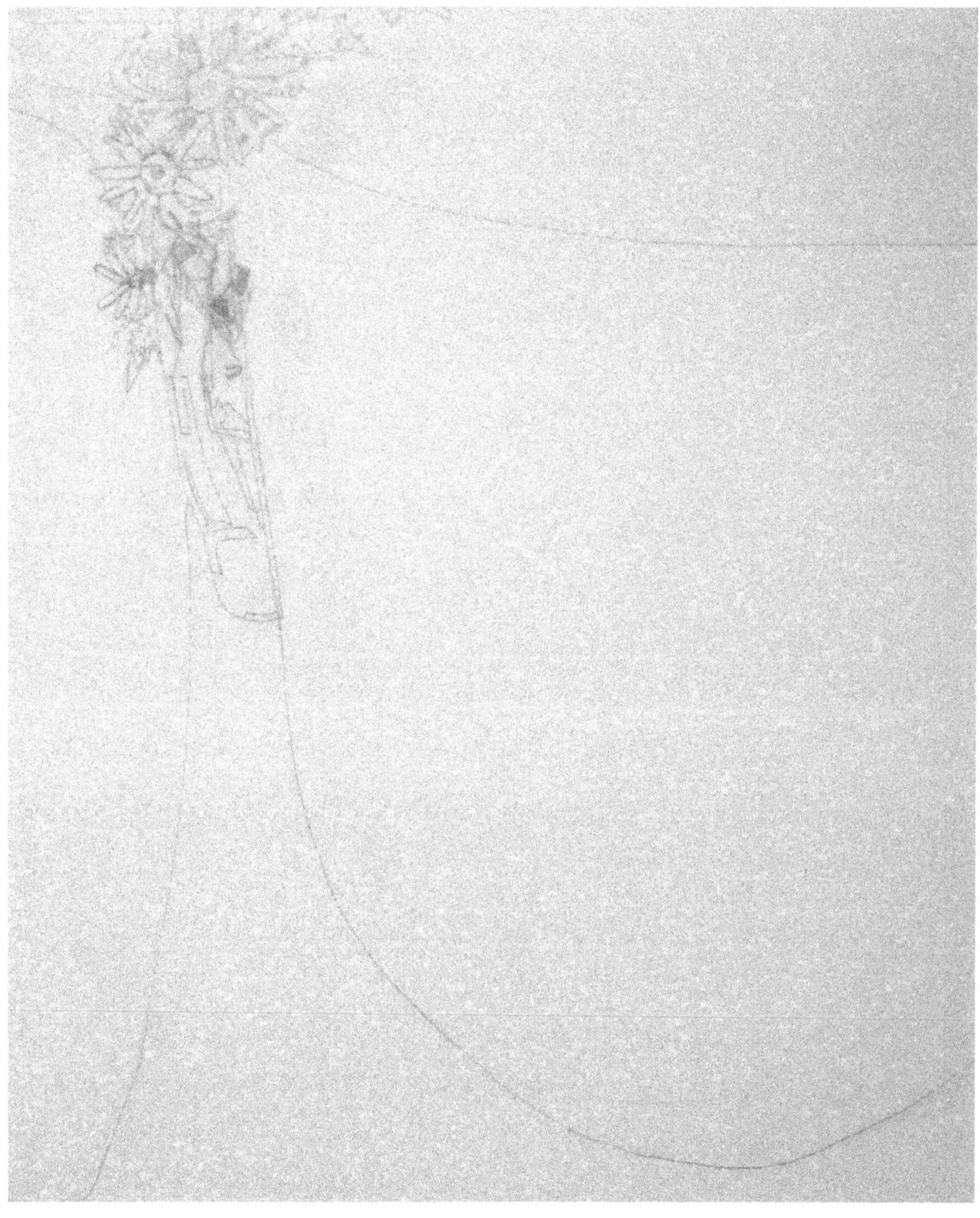

Amy Watson

2/26/16, 6:50 p.m.
13. Finished all the other detail. Ready for the bangs which should be straight lines. Got locked out, since I had difficulty turning the key and had someone help me. Hope I have better luck next time. Maybe I was too nervous. Going home to have a ziti dinner my boyfriend made.

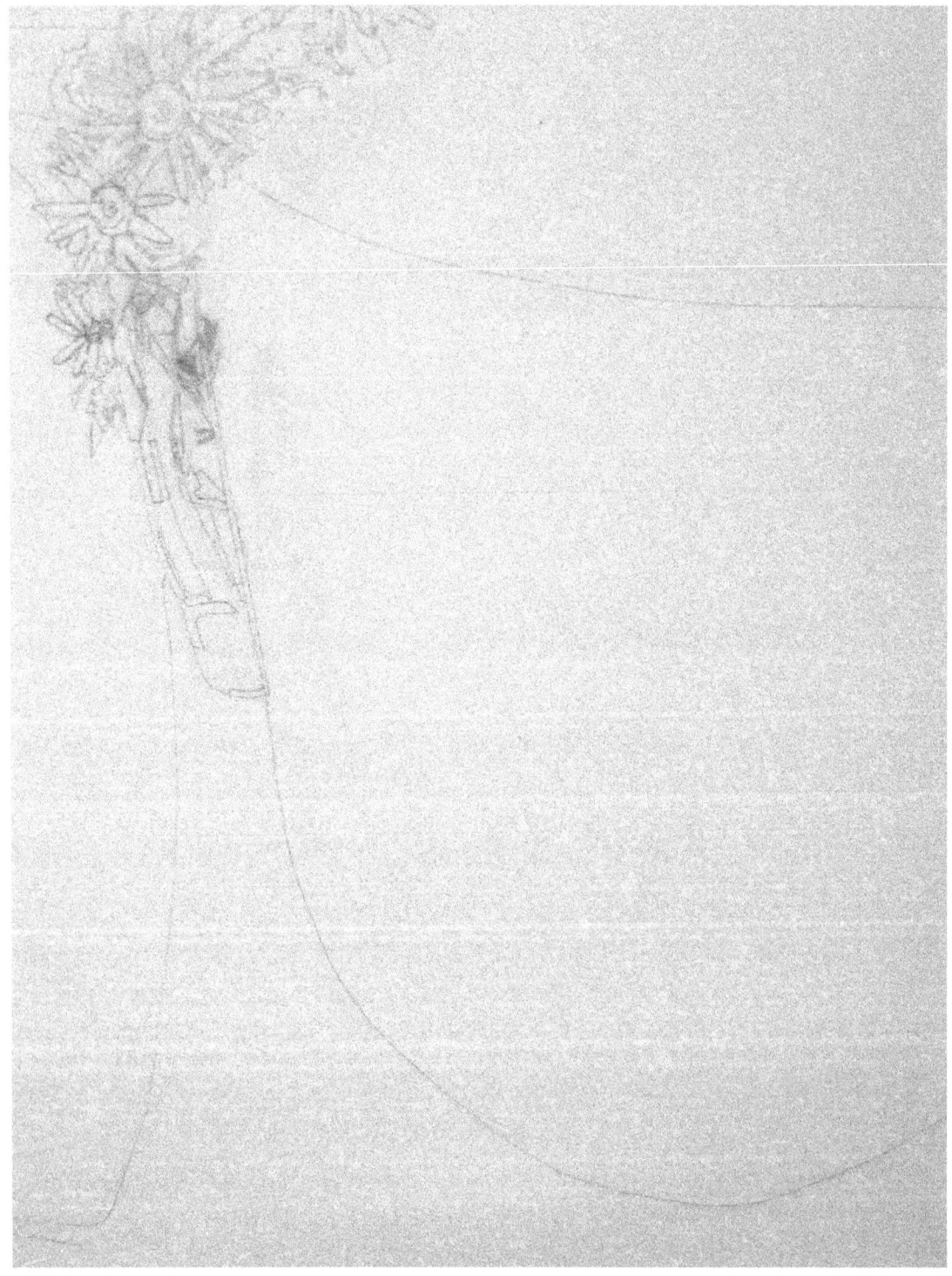

2/27/16, 9:55 p.m.
 14. Completed the shadow of the flower. Almost completed the bangs. Finished the side burn. Came late because had migraine and was on the computer shopping. Horrible accident near home when I left yesterday. Delicious dinner.

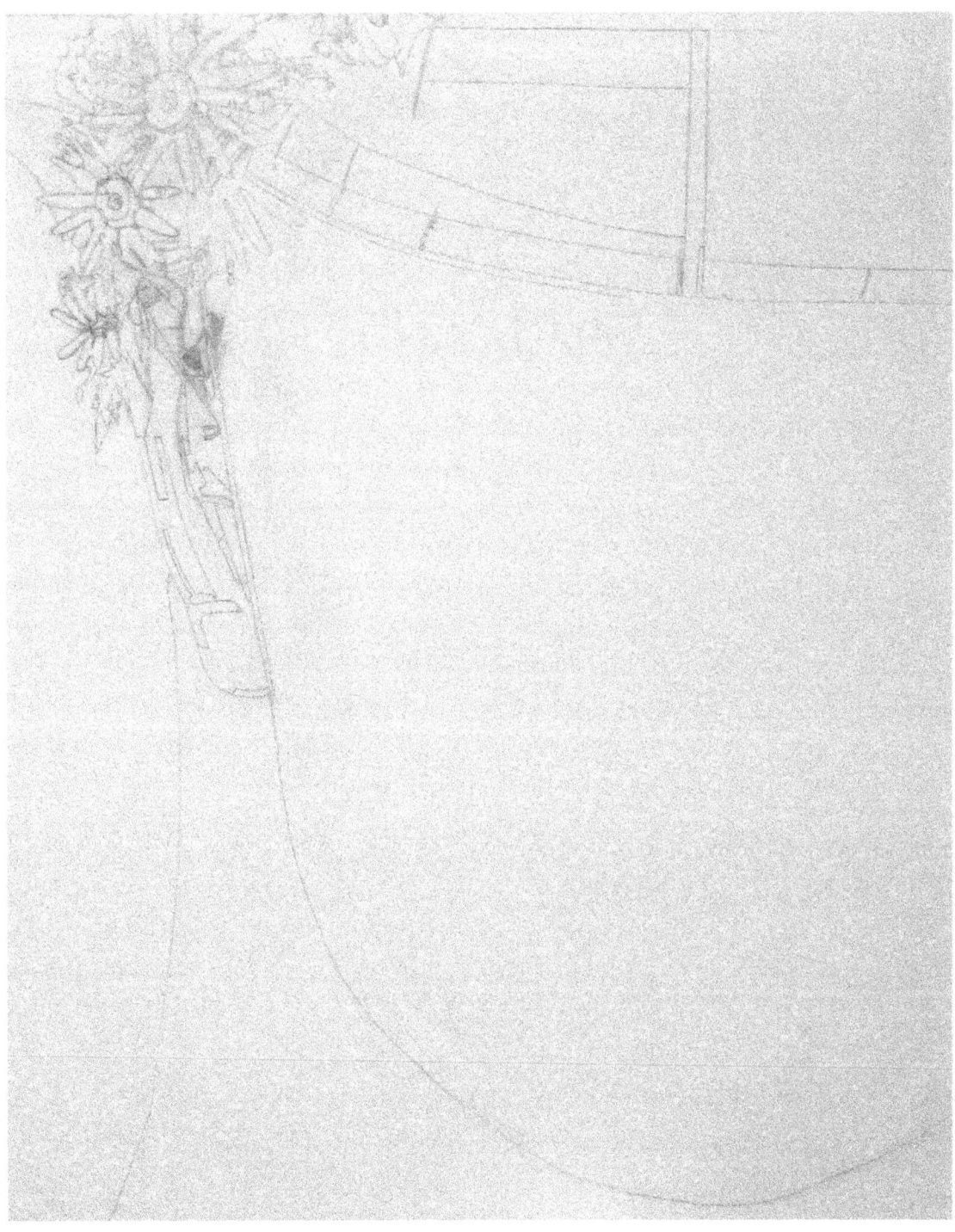

Amy Watson

2/28/16, 8:10 p.m.
15. Completed the bangs and eyebrows almost. Started nose, but too low. Began shading around the eye. Will continue tomorrow. Walked 3 circles today. A cop was on the side. Had too many teas. My boyfriend called about what time I would be home to have dinner. Before I left he was on the back road in his friend's vehicle with him and his friend hanging out. I had to go back there to ask where the cream was for the tea.

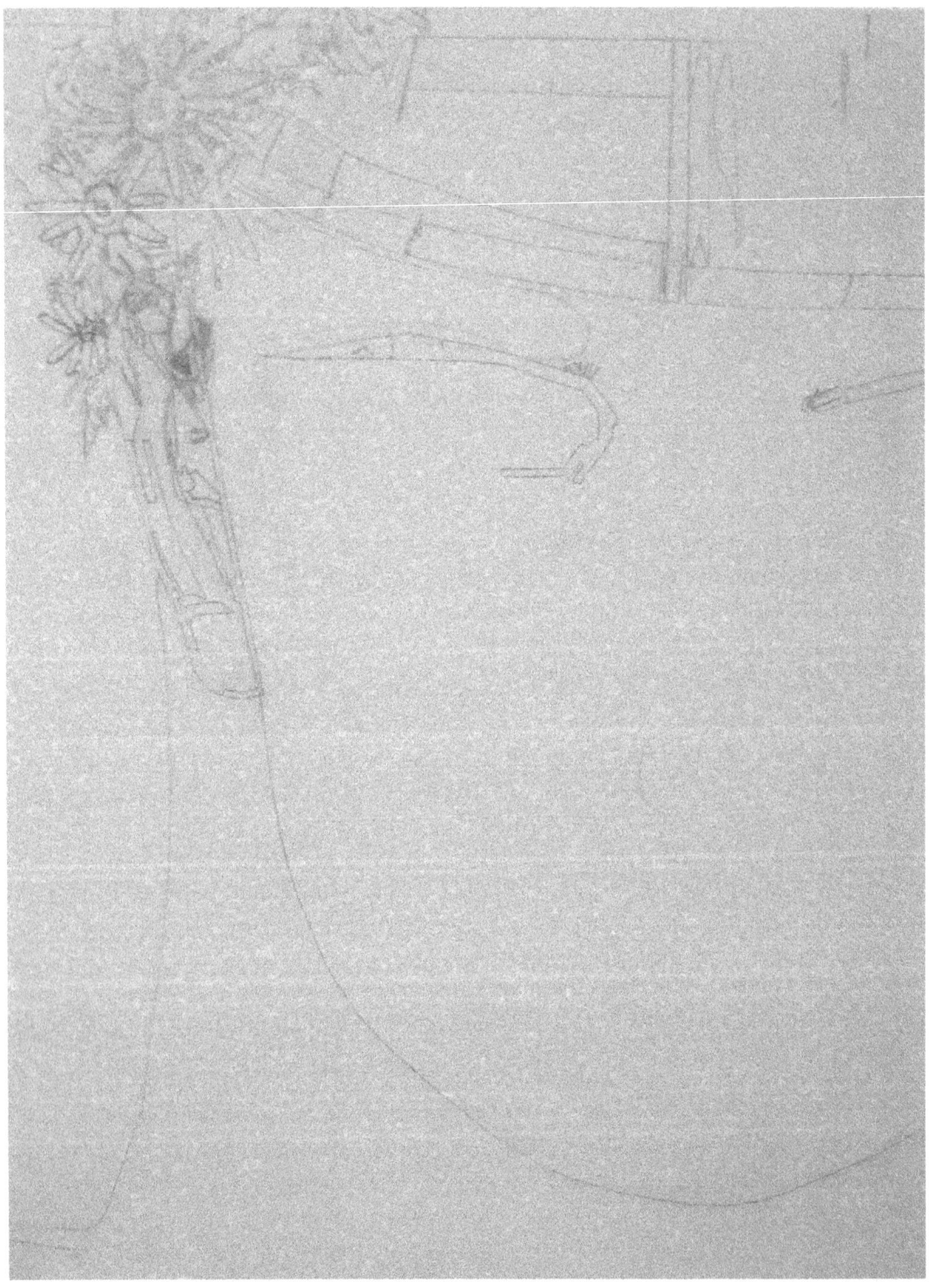

2/29/16 5:35 p.m.
16. Another bad accident as I was going home last night. Finished one eye. Started on second. Completed second eyebrow. Also finished shading under first eye. Had trouble getting the first eye just the right shape. I think they are too small and look almond shaped, so the child won't look cute, but we'll see once I complete the full nose. There's so much more to cover on the bottom of the face.

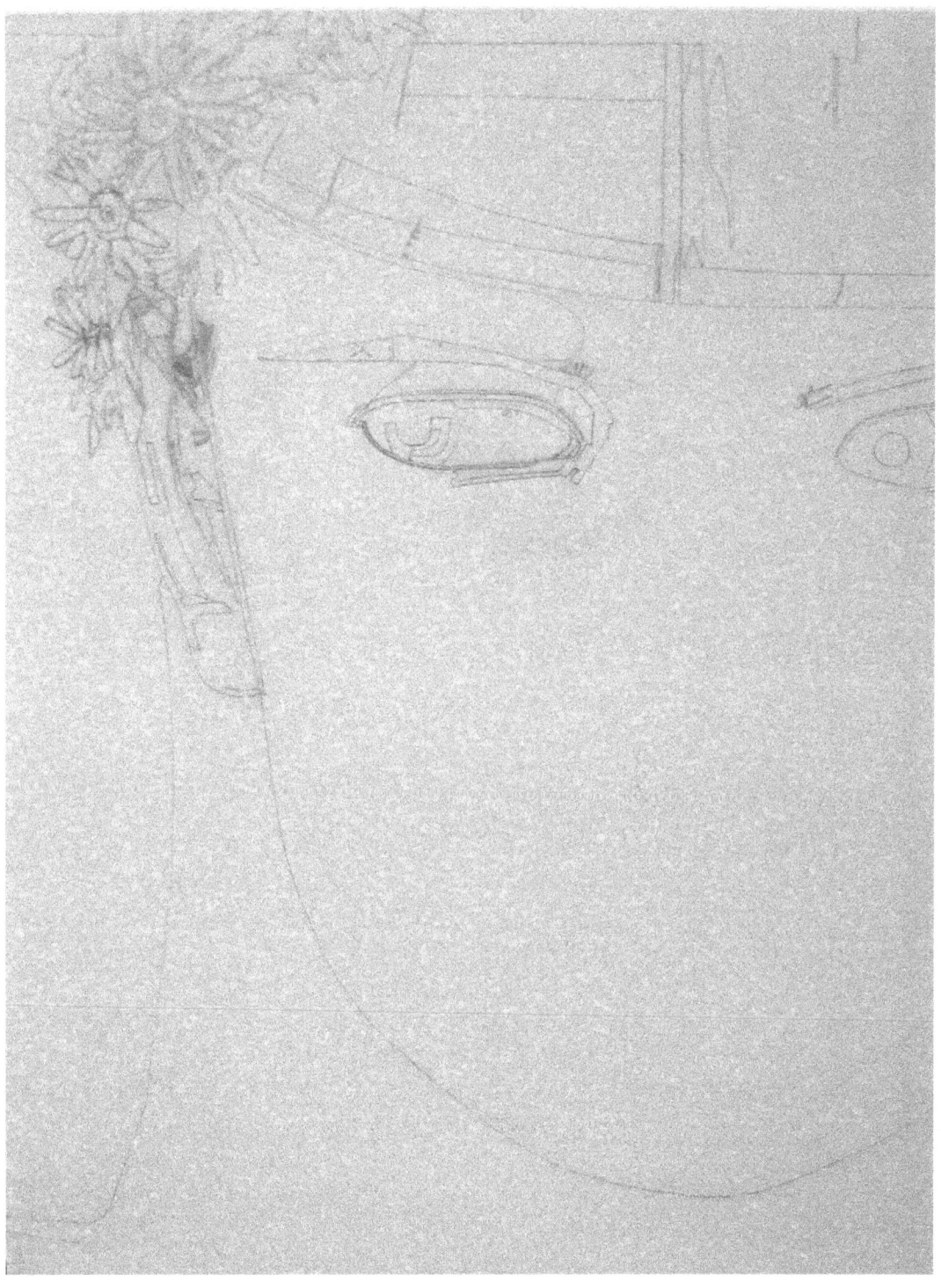

Amy Watson

3/1/16, 5:25 p.m.
17. Didn't spend much time here today, but need more pencils anyway. Completed second eye. Started shading for nose. Battery is dead. Took some pictures with fur. Don't need bed. Sink will be fixed.

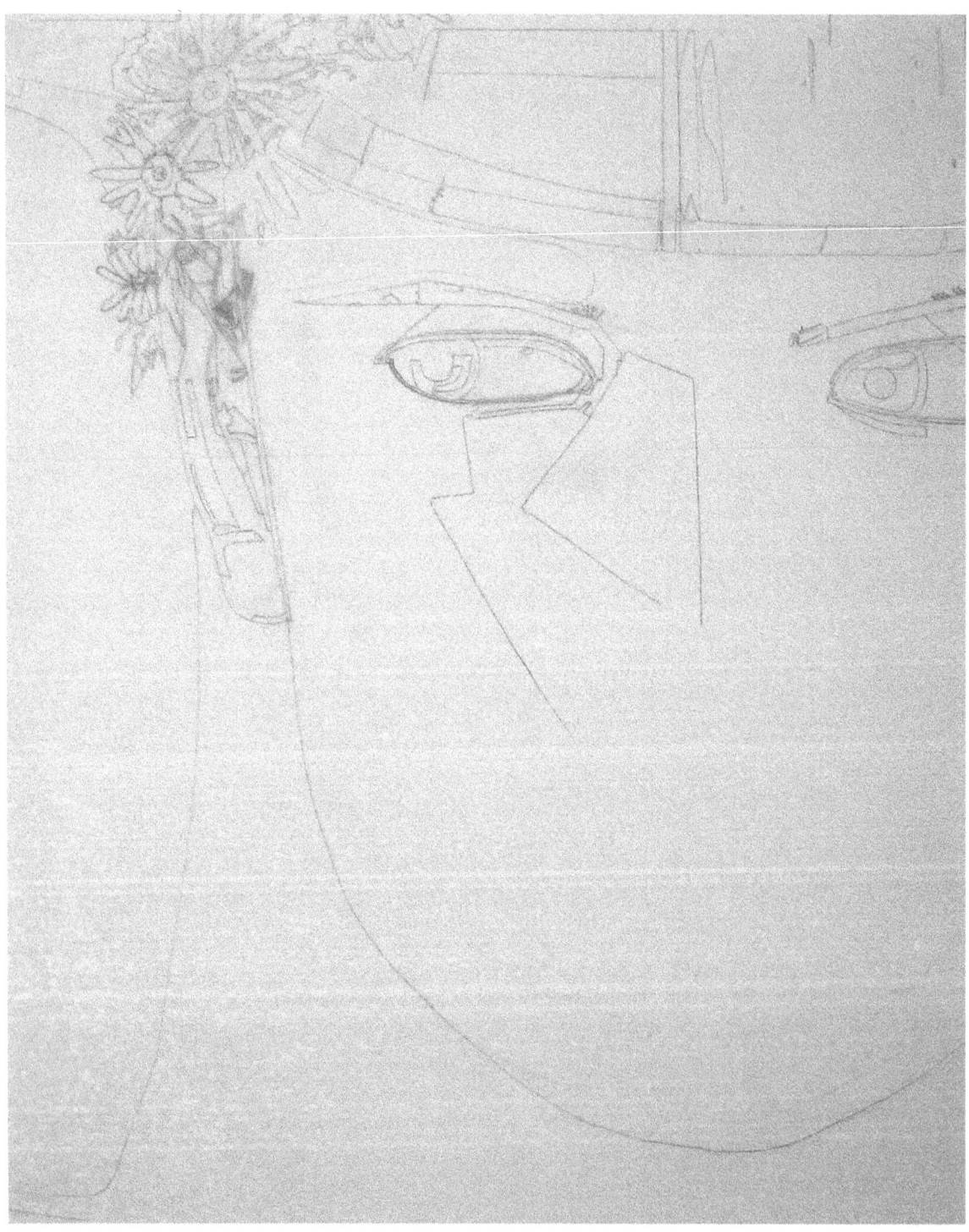

3/2/16, 6:40 p.m.
18. Finished the shading in the hair and began with the neck. Started with the nose. Didn't feel well today, so didn't get as much done as I wanted, since I relaxed a lot. The sink still isn't fixed. Will arrive early tomorrow to pay rent.

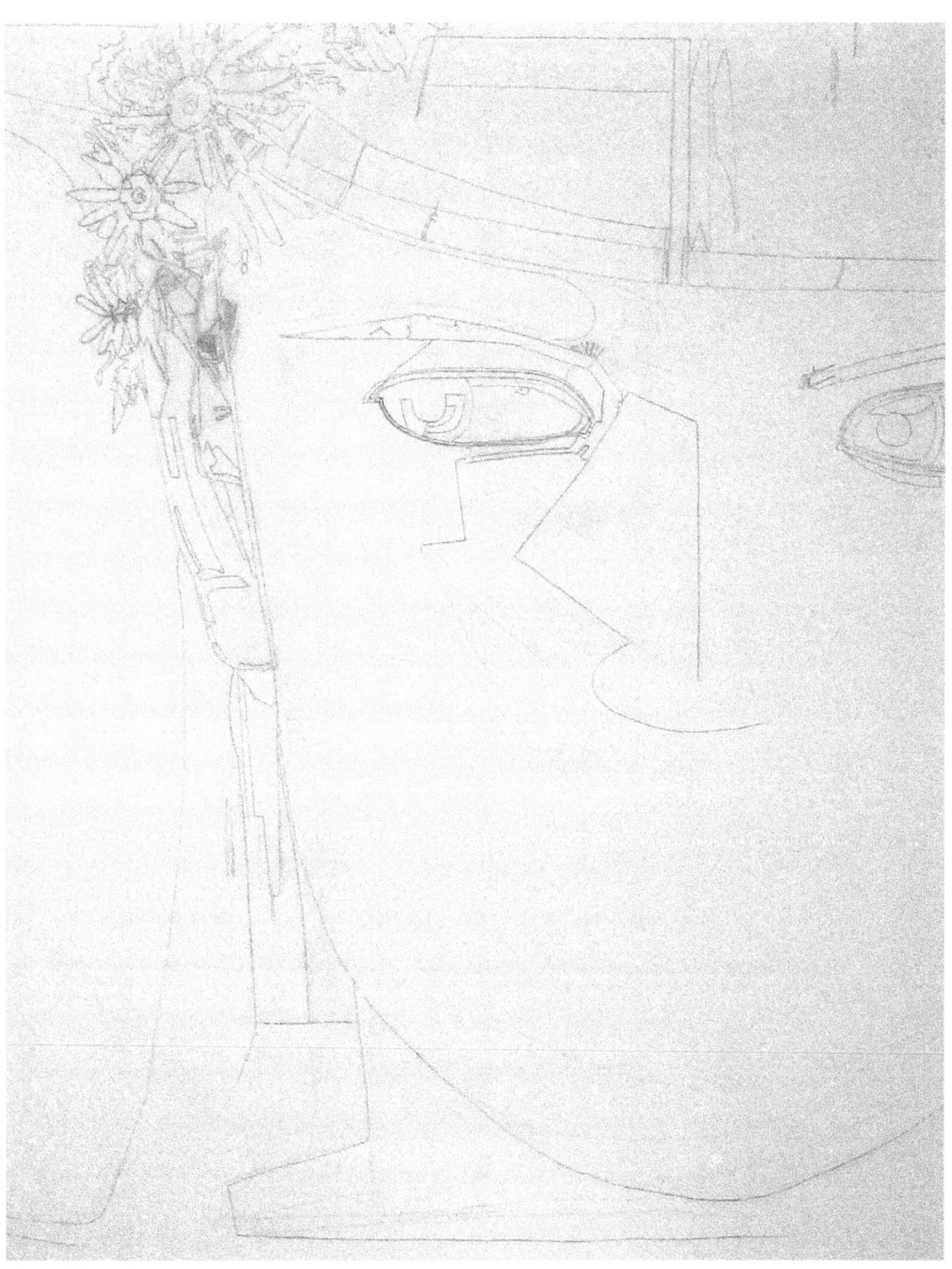

Amy Watson

3/3/16, 8:30 p.m.
19. Finished shading the left side of the face. Finished creating the shape of the nose and began shading around it. Created first hole in nose. Went shopping and didn't feel well so didn't get as much done as I wanted. I'm glad I found some shades of paint on sale for the face.

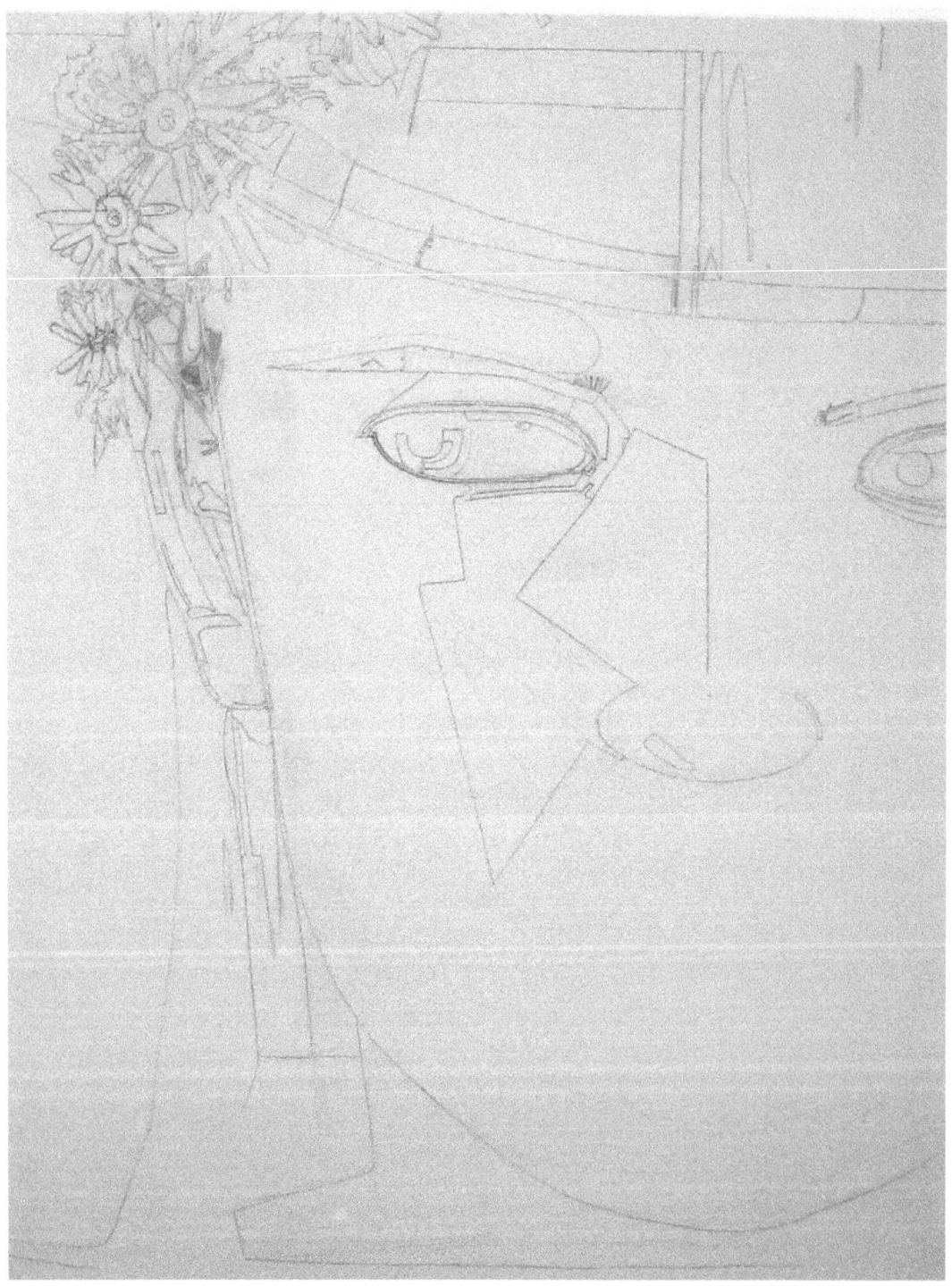

3/4/16, 8:40 p.m.
20. Finished the nose. Finished the shading on the right side of the nose and created lines for shading. Created right cheek. Created shadow above right eyebrow. The nose took a lot of time. Got here later.

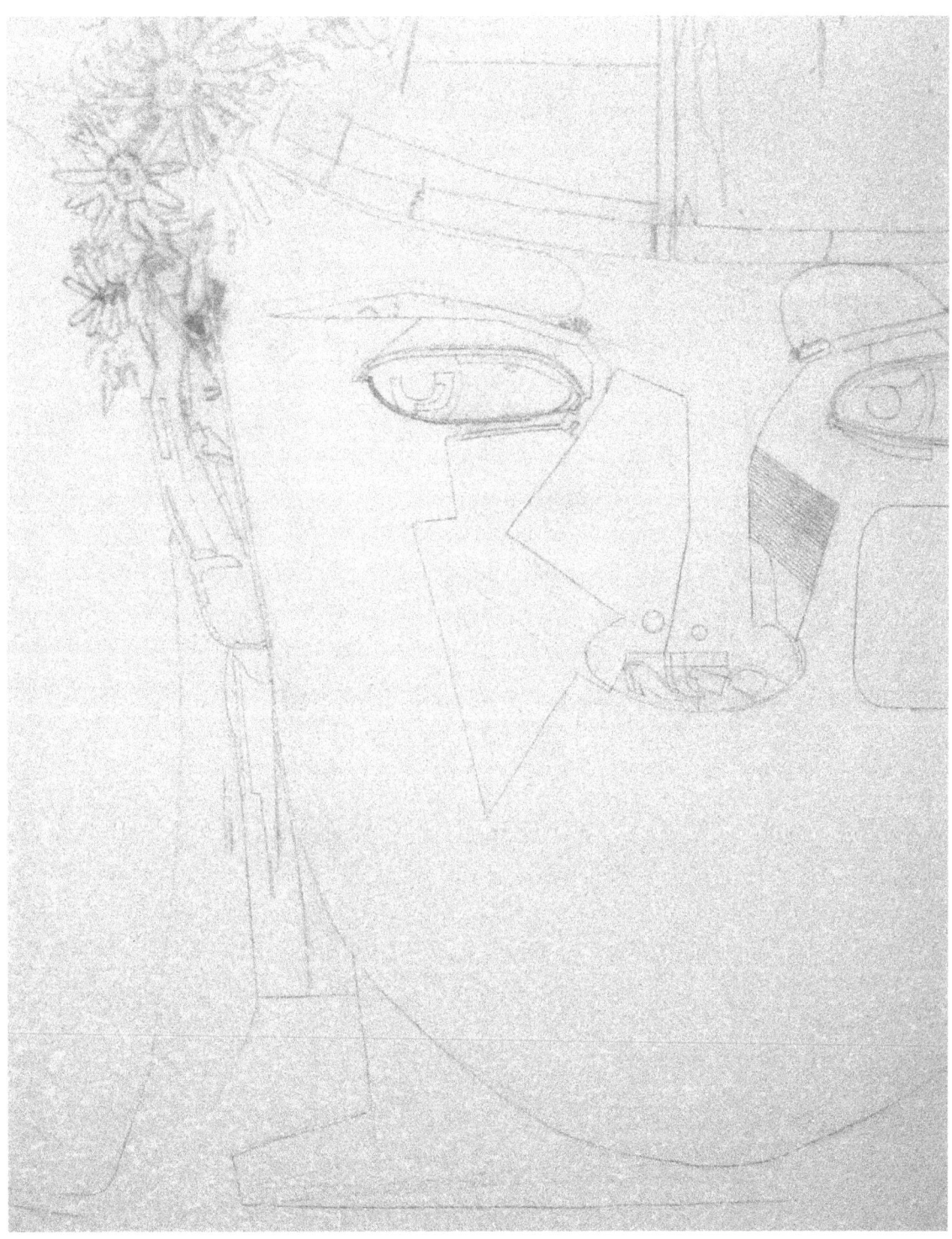

Amy Watson

3/5/16, 5:15 p.m.
21. I drew lines under the nose and areas for shading. I drew the lips and the crease line. I drew the areas inside for shading. I began drawing the areas on the left side for shading. I took a short video to capture it.

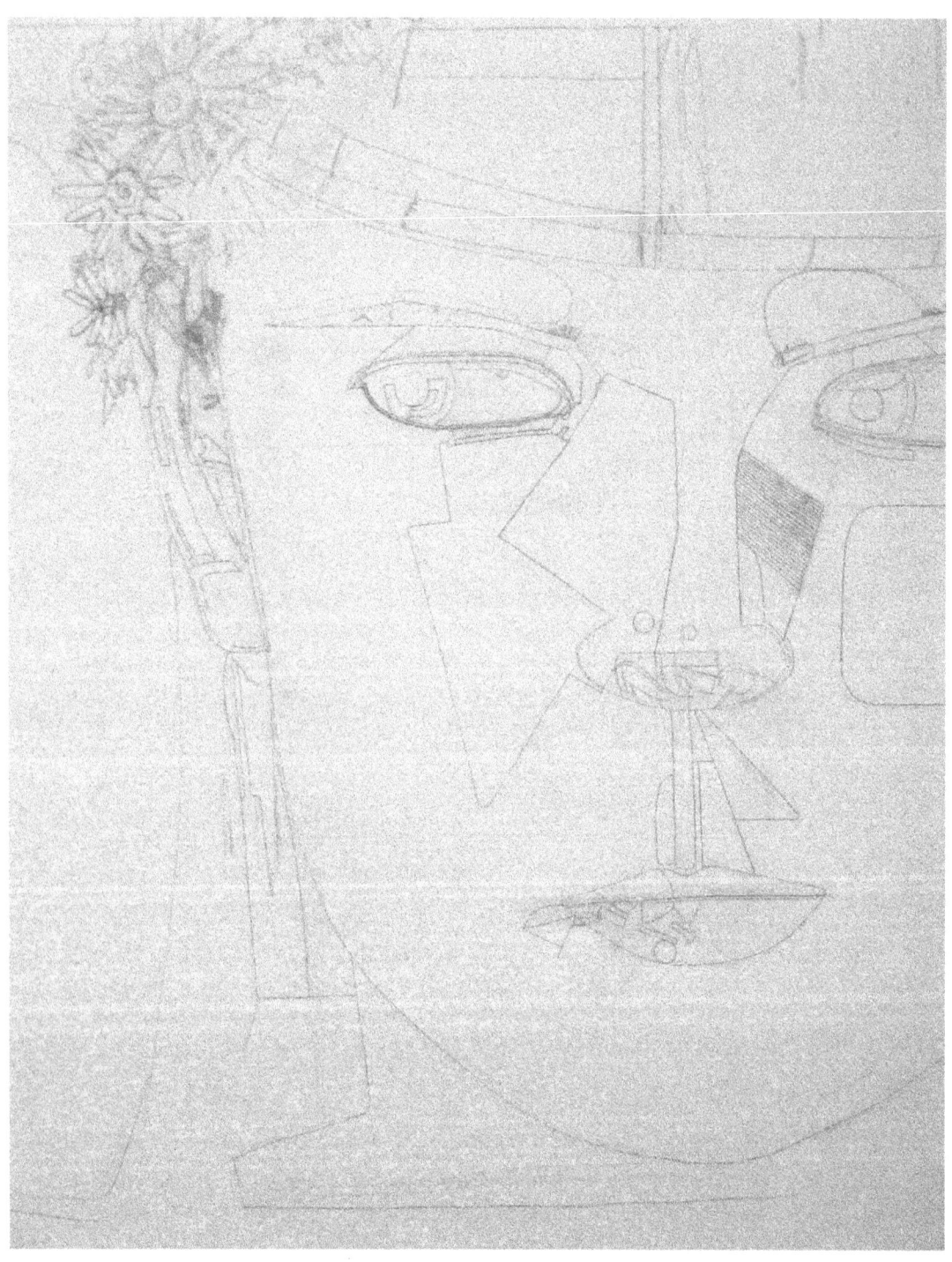

How To Draw and Paint Amelia

3/6/16, 7:20 p.m.
22. Finished the mouth-the inside and the shading on the outside. Completed shading under the chin. Drew the head for the mermaid which is the last part. My legs hurt, so I will leave. Brought paints. Someone is playing live music. Ate Subway.

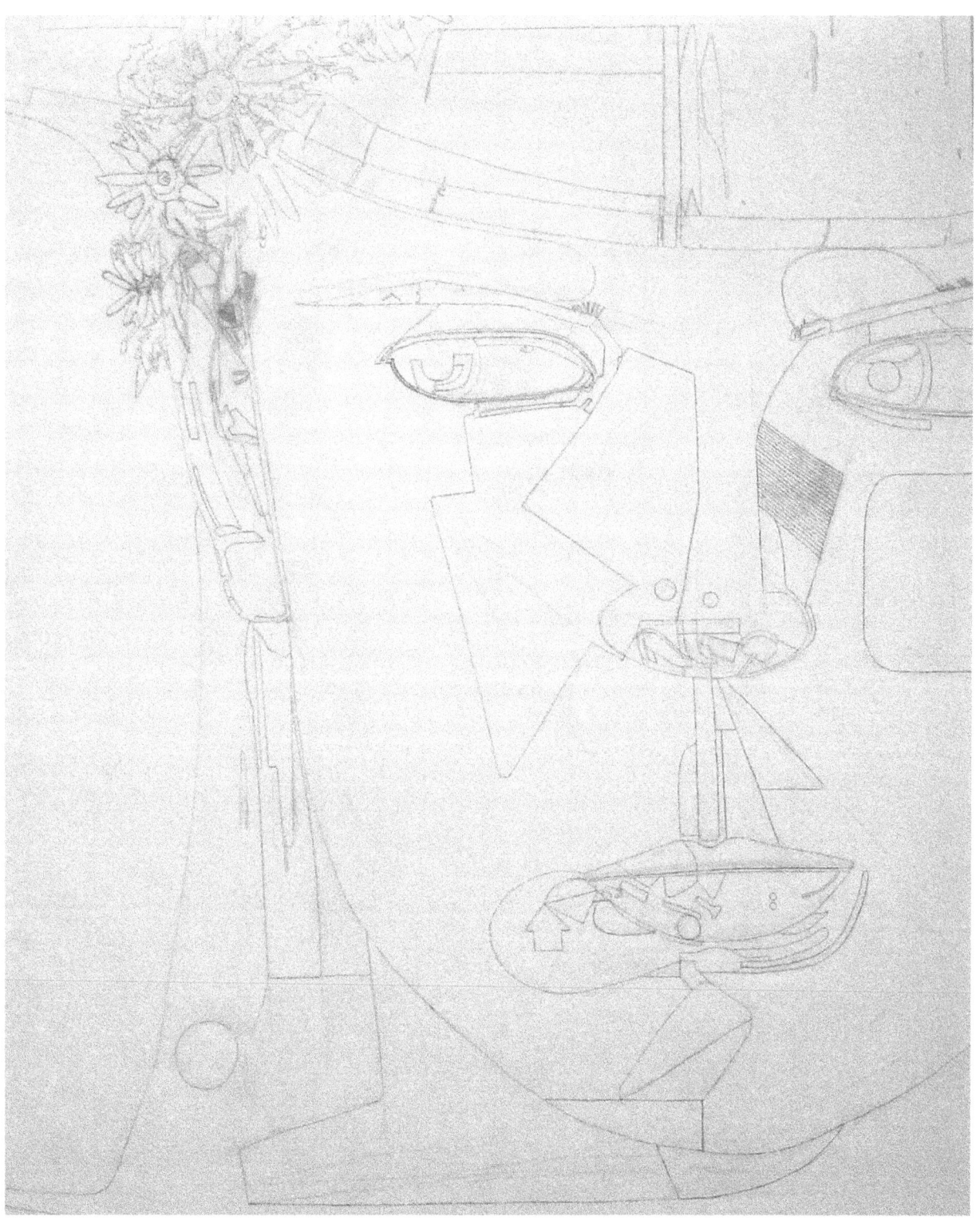

Amy Watson

3/7/16, 5:20 p.m.
23. Finished mermaid which I started today except for the round circle for the head. The left arm was too low so I moved it up. I began painting the white daisies and was disappointed that the new white paint turned clear.

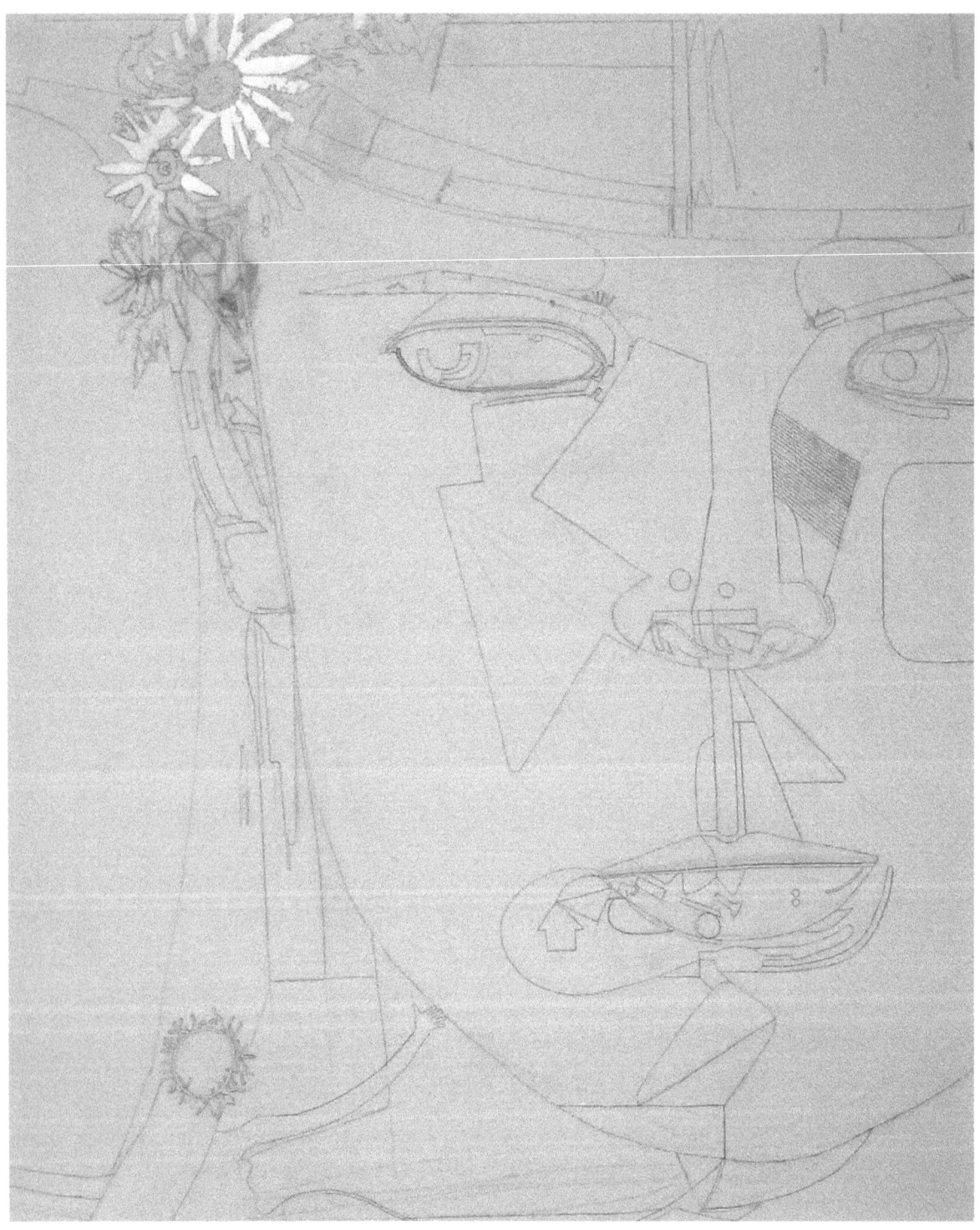

3/8/16, 8:30 p.m.
   24. Painted white in eyes. Painted one eye gray. Painted left side of painting beige along with the mermaid's hair and the corner on the right side. I got here much later today and walked.

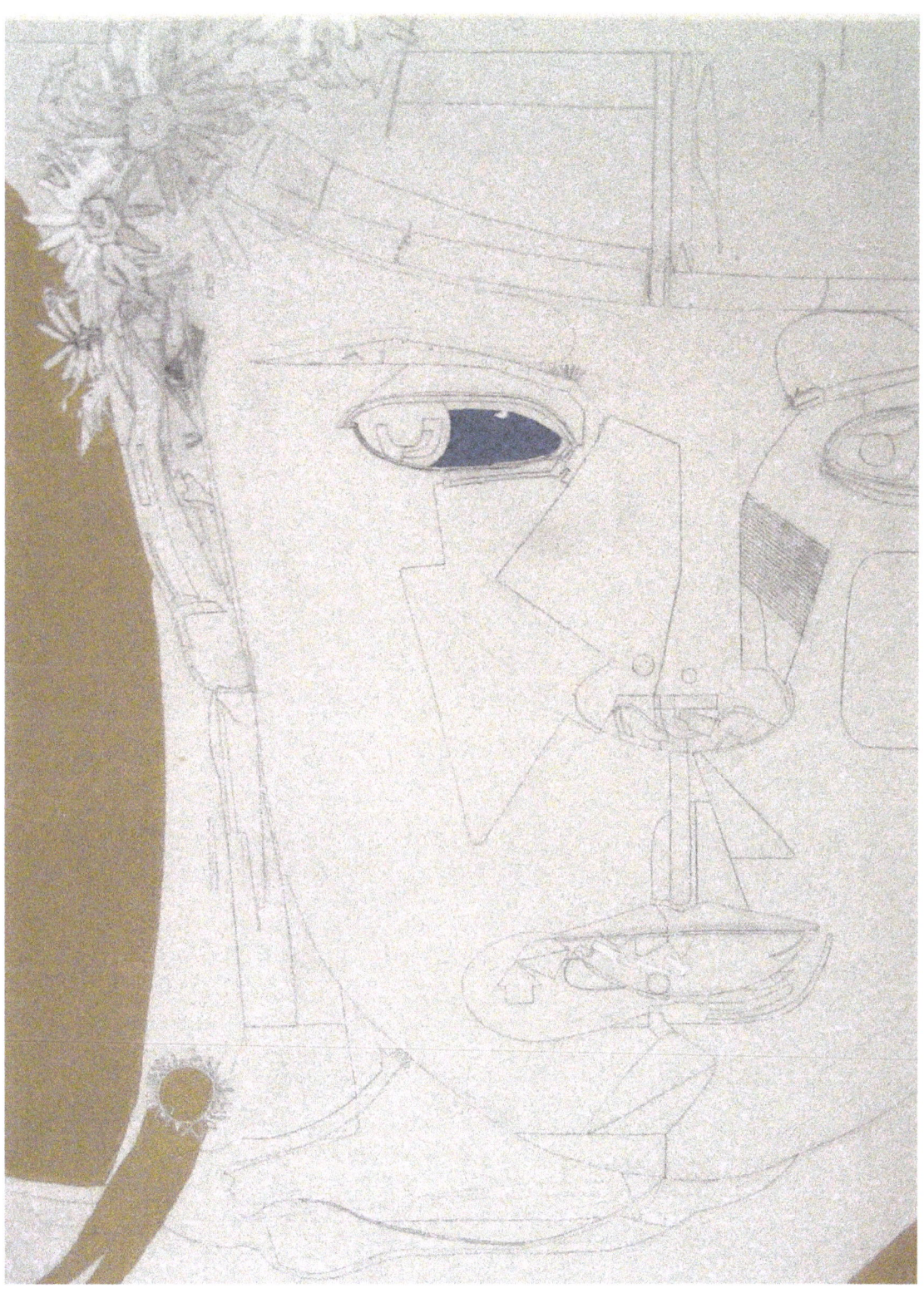

Amy Watson

3/9/16, 7:15 p.m.
25. Did detail in the flowers. Changed the shade to the eye to silver, since I forgot that I bought the new paint. Shaded the left side of the face. Spent a lot of time here. Hopefully will get hot water soon. Walked 30 minutes since it was a beautiful day.

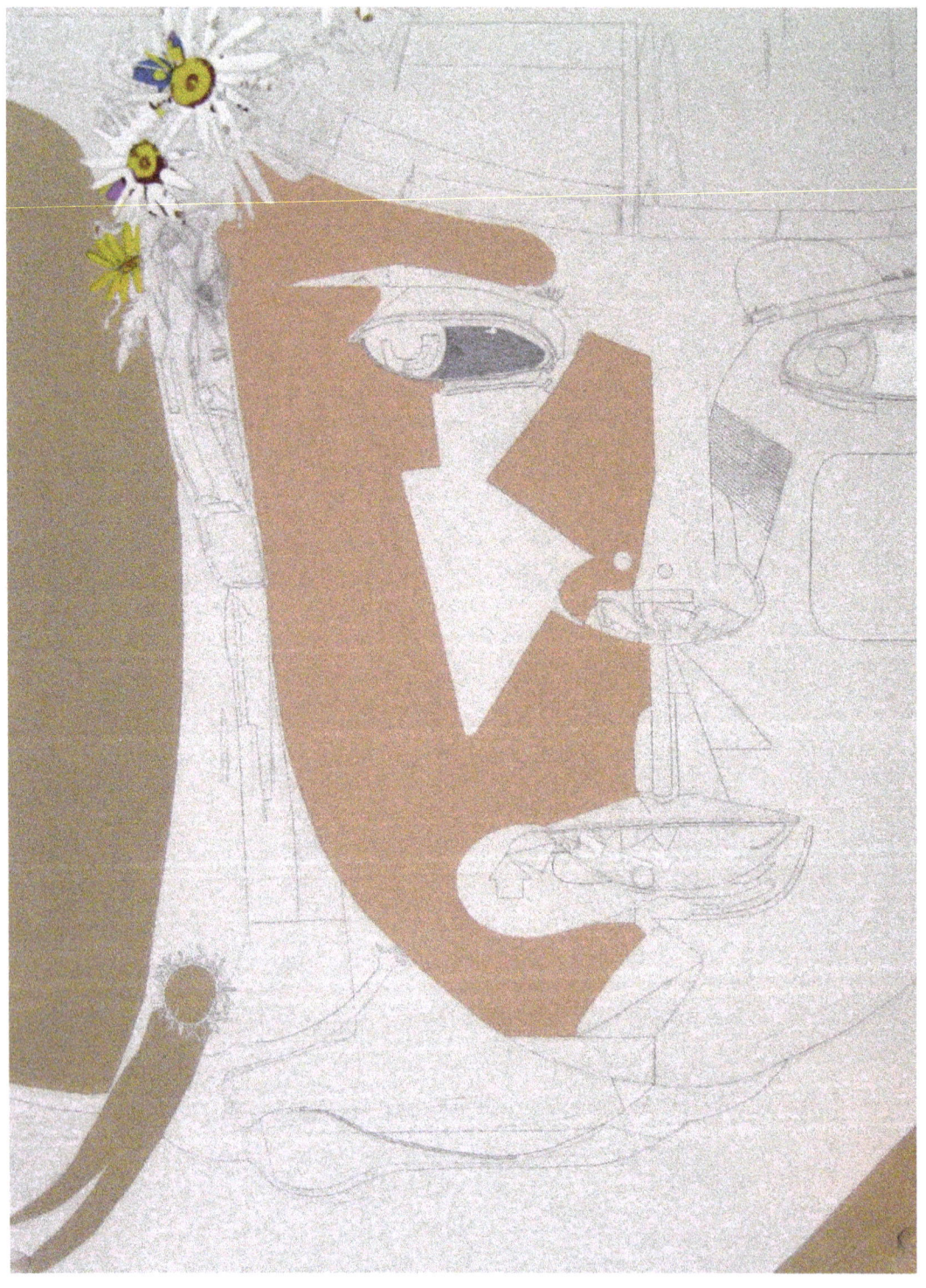

3/10/16, 9:05 p.m.
26. Finished painting nude color under the nose and the ear. Finished painting beige color on right side of the face. I like how the textures are different. Painted in the stripes. Painted large shadow under chin.

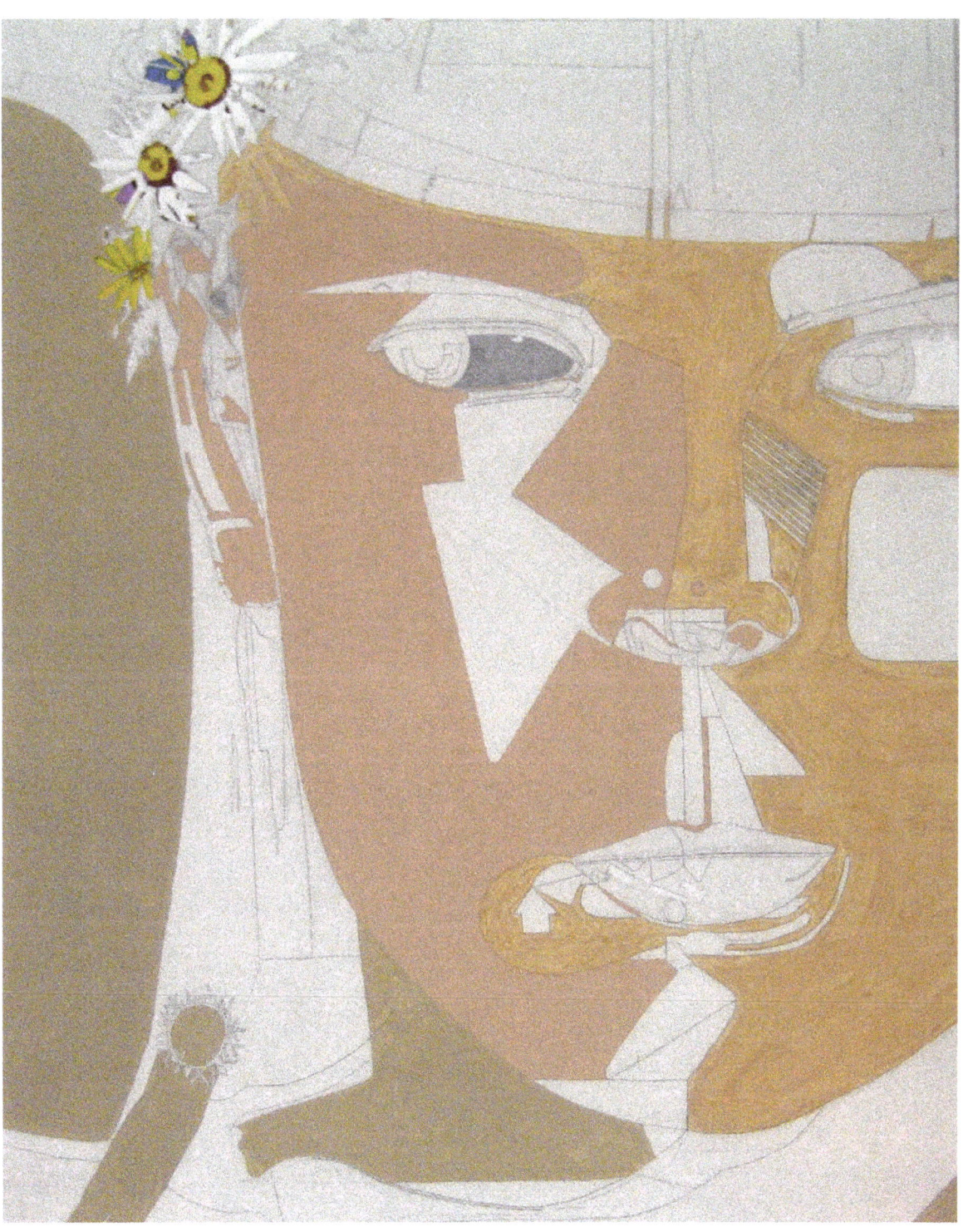

Amy Watson

3/11/16, 9:15 p.m.
27. I completely finished the shading on the nose, on the side of it, and underneath. I also finished the shading on the left side of the lip and underneath it.

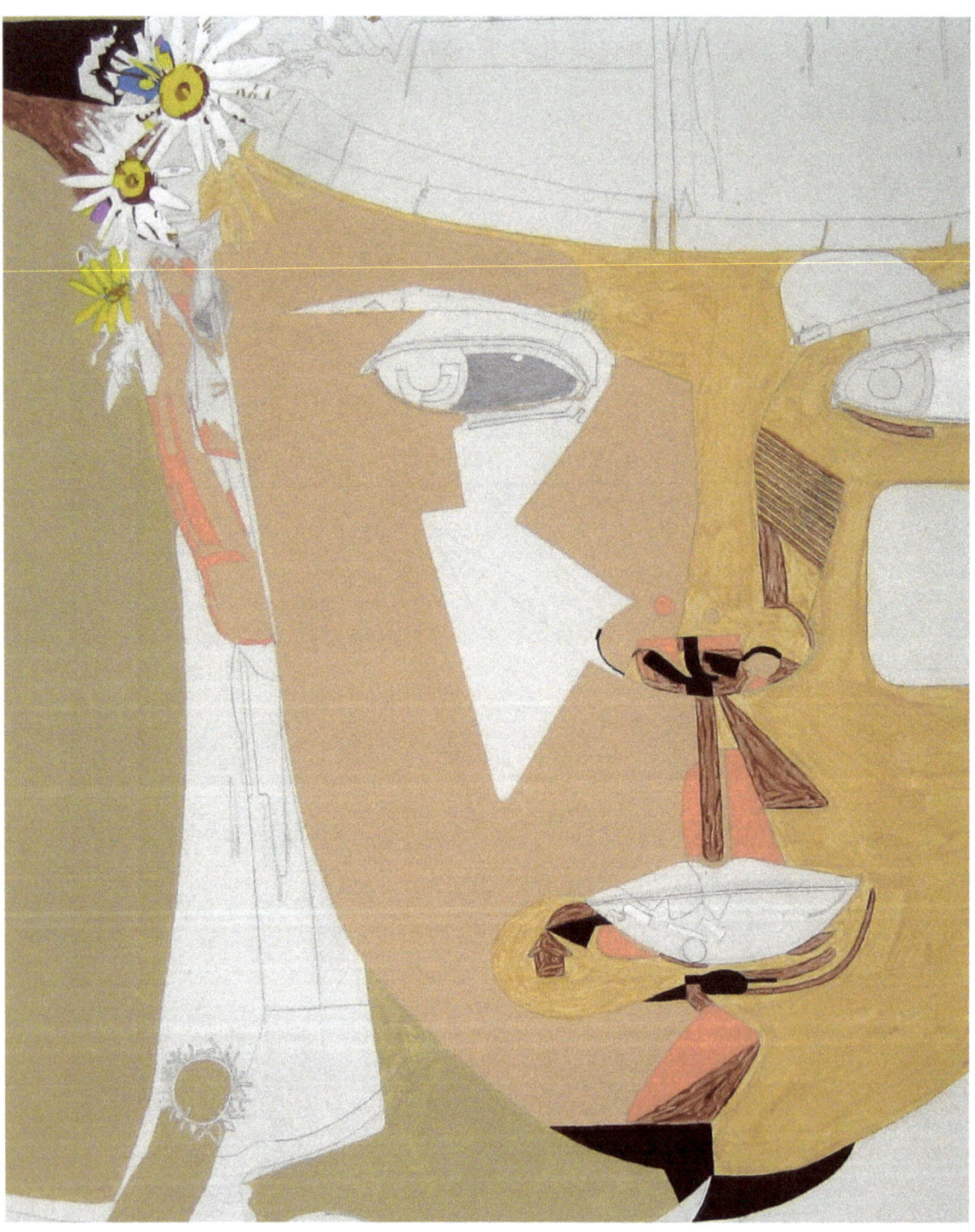

3/12/16, 8:50 p.m.
28. I came later today and got meatloaf with mashed potatoes at Boston Market. I did the hair in 4 colors on the bangs and on the left side. I also did shading above the right eye. I walked 30 minutes before I started, finished my raspberry tea, had a water, and then a coffee with hazelnut creamer later. For snacks I had a fruit roll up and peanut butter granola bar.

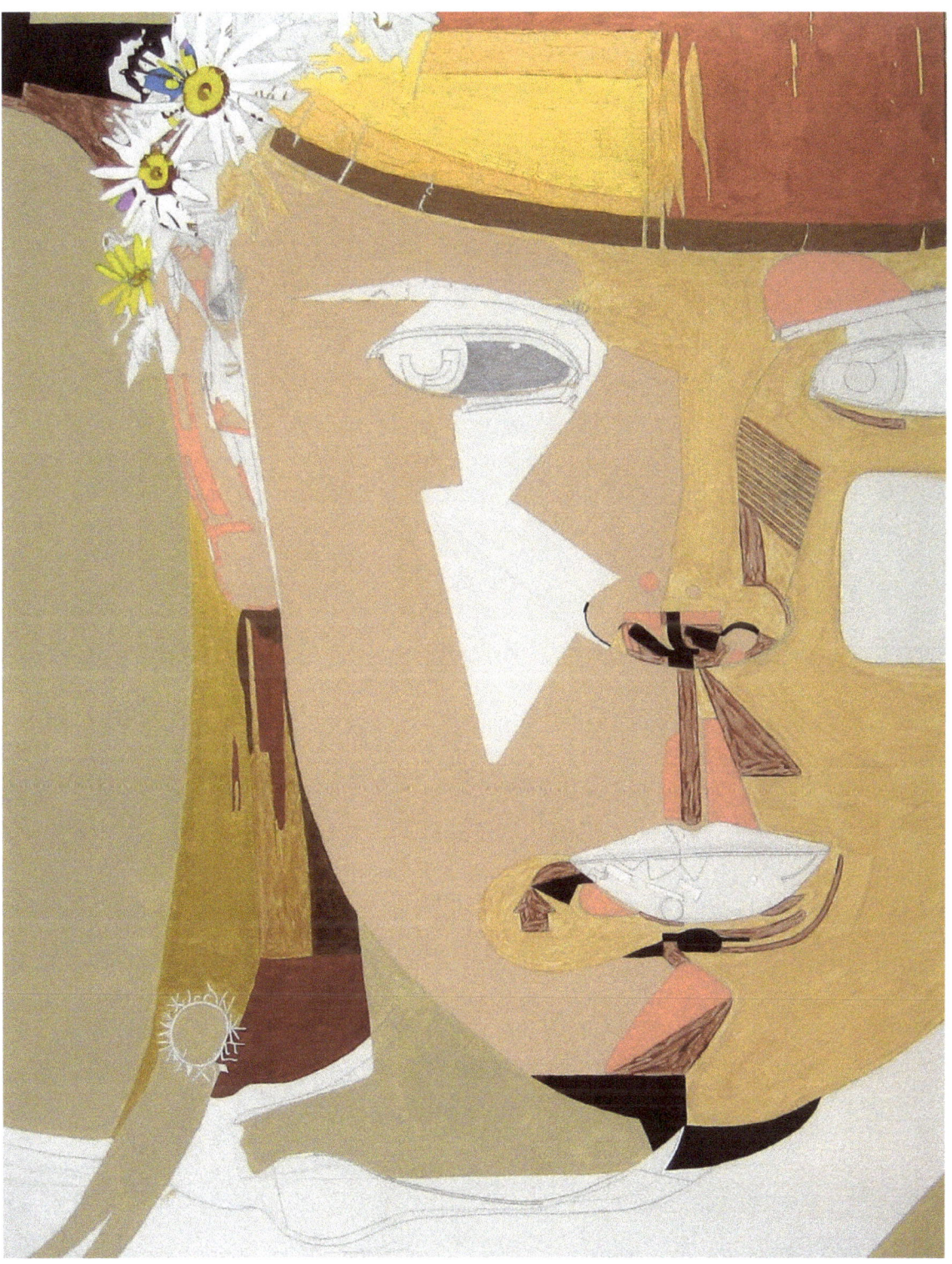

Amy Watson

3/13/16, 9:50 p.m.

29. Only spent a couple of hours here because we lost an hour. I actually came here and left since my boyfriend needed the car. I ran errands before hand and walked 30 minutes. I bought little cups to put left over paint. I listened to Bob Marley and the Beatles. I filled in around the flowers brown, since it looked empty. I went down to the ear. I filled in the empty space on the bottom of the mermaid. I was debating a dark brown like the shadow.

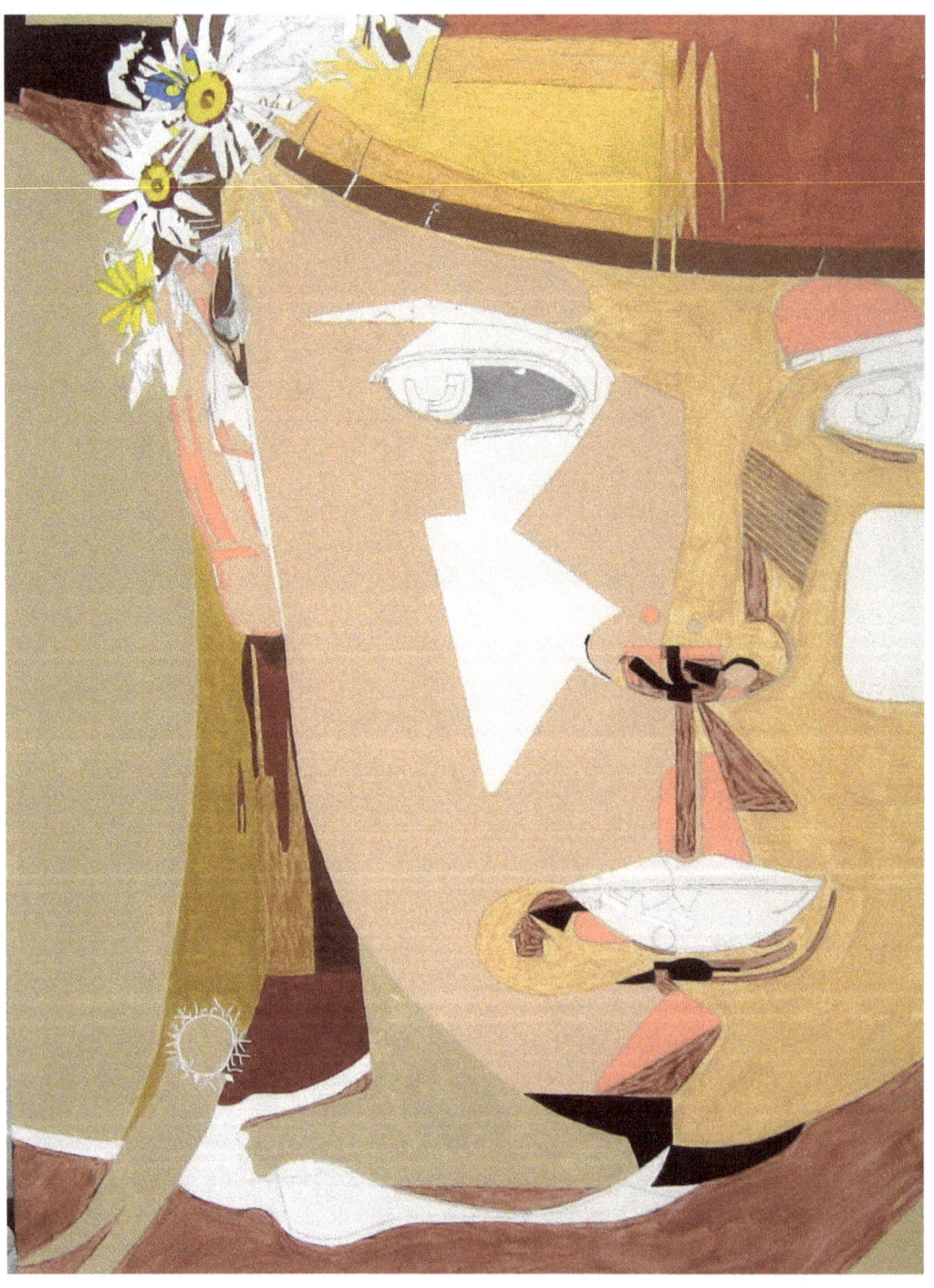

3/14/16, 7:40 p.m.
30. I painted the shadows of the yellow daisy pink. I painted the left cheek orange red and the right one slightly darker. I painted the lips the same color as the left cheek. I painted the shadows of the lips red and the outline of the mermaid.

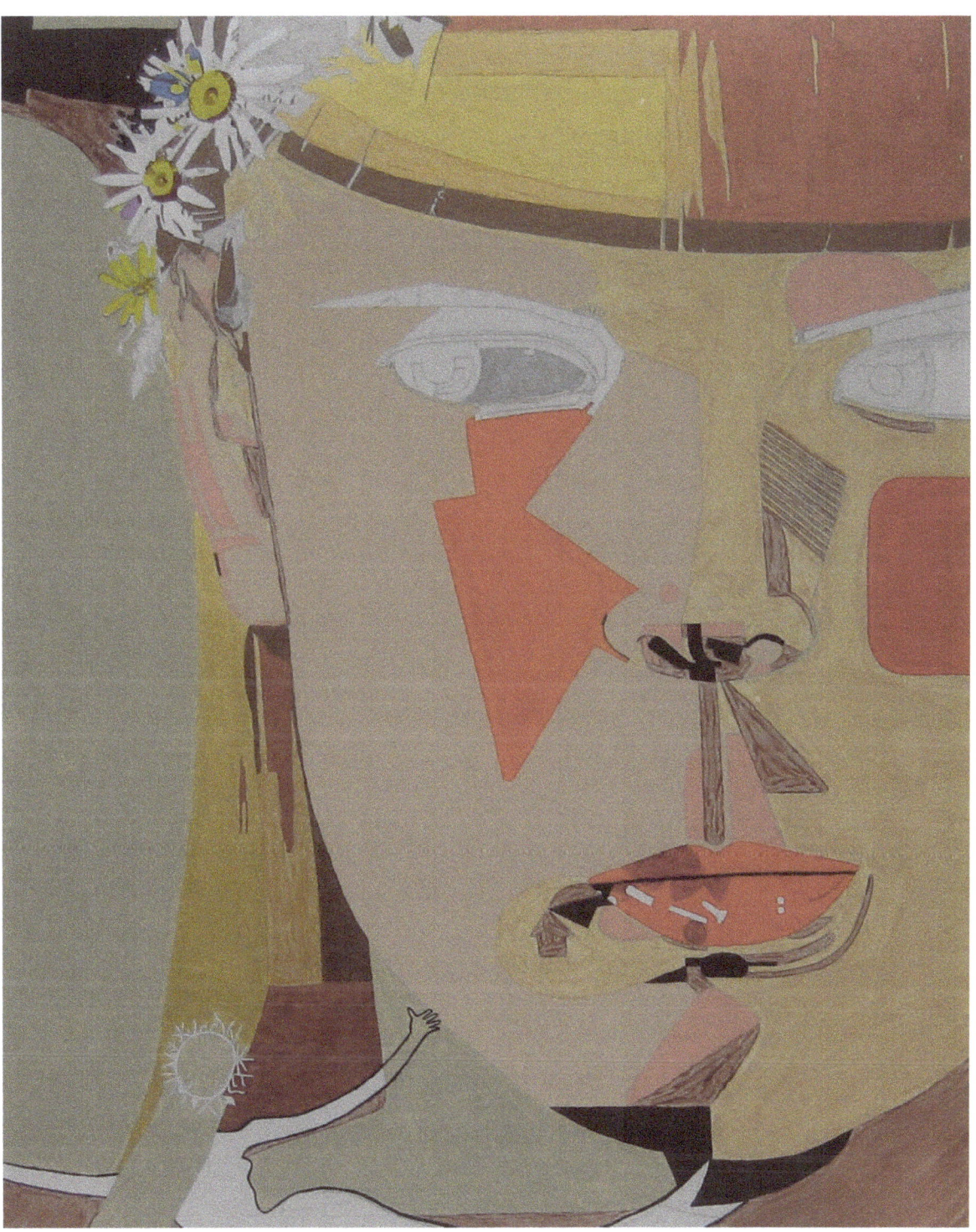

Amy Watson

3/15/16, 9:40 p.m.
   31. I painted the crown in the mermaid's hair. I also painted the mermaid brown and green inside. I painted the hair gold near the ear and touched it up near the crown. I also touched up the beige near the crown and the hand.

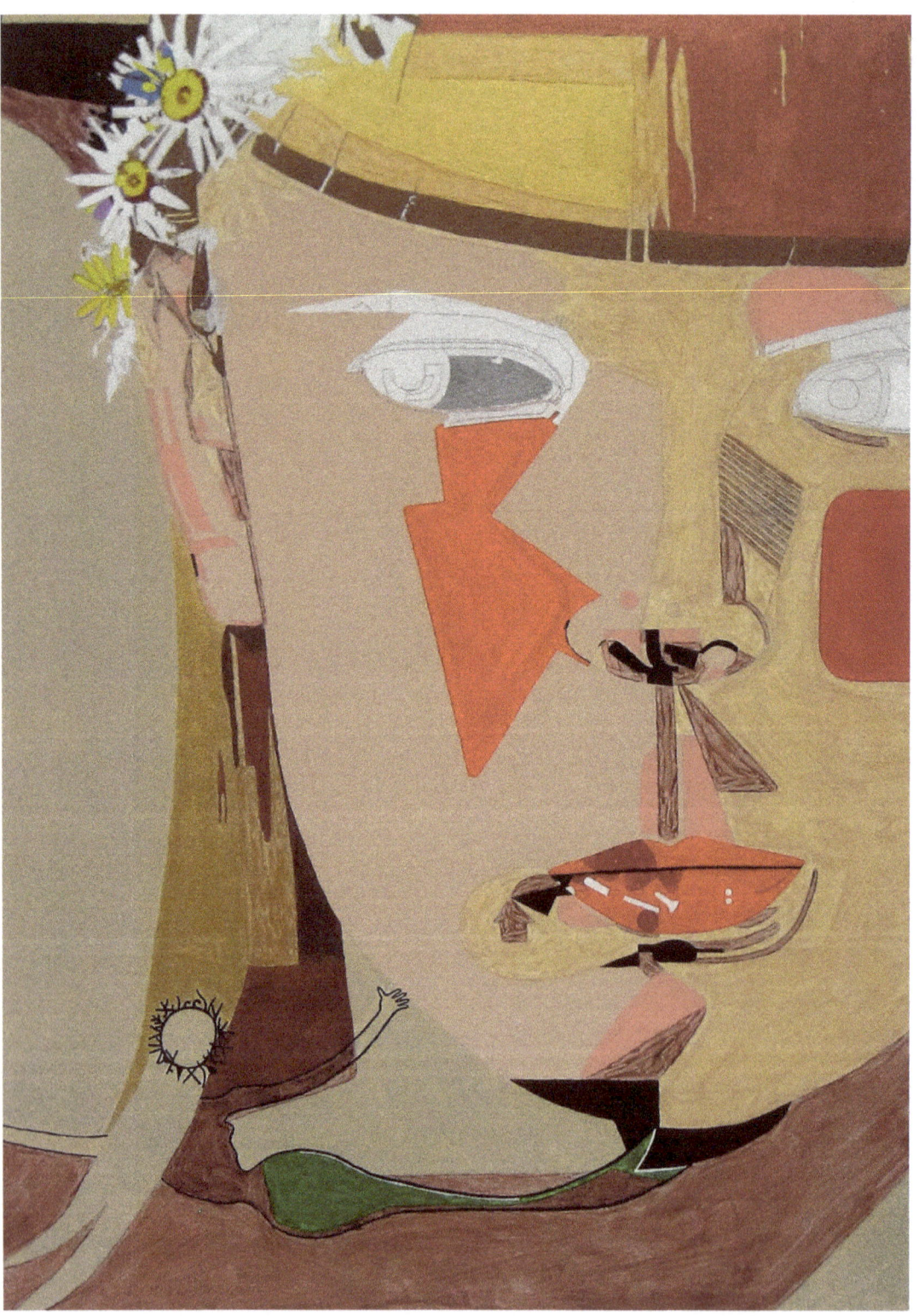

3/16/17, 8:45 p.m.
  32. I finished the eyeballs, eyelids, above the eye and below the eyes with shading. I changed the right eyeball to a lighter blue. I completed the eyebrows. I painted the leaves green.

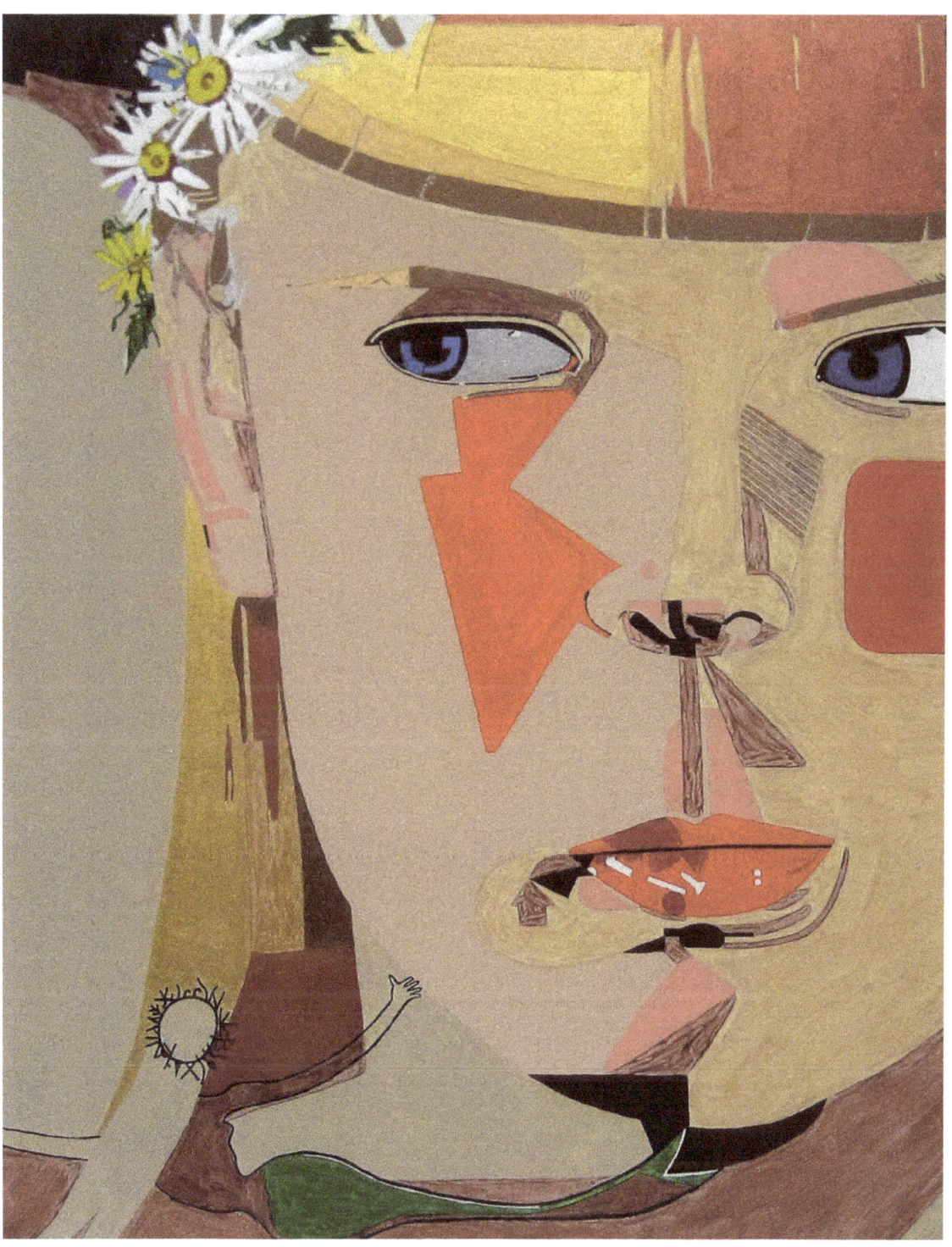

Amy Watson

3/17/16, 6:20 p.m.
33. I completed the details in the flowers. I was late arriving to my Mom's for corned beef and cabbage. She said she would like to hang the painting.

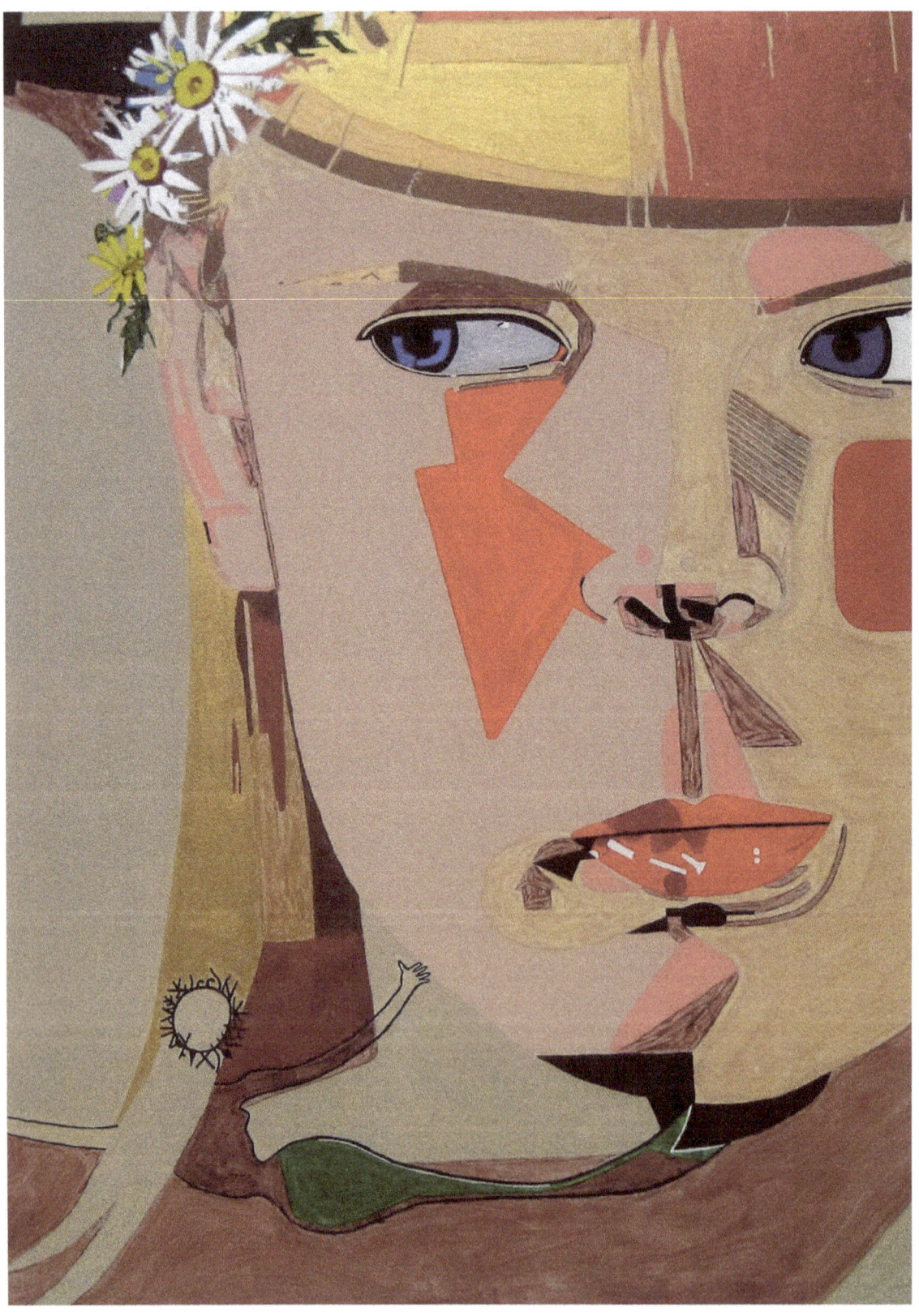

3/18/16
34. I signed my name. I bought another canvas the same size previously and went down to pick it up because of the rain, but it rained again. It almost fit completely in my trunk and it didn't get ruined. I also have been buying discounted supplies for my next project if I see them. I also put the title of the painting and date on the back in pen.

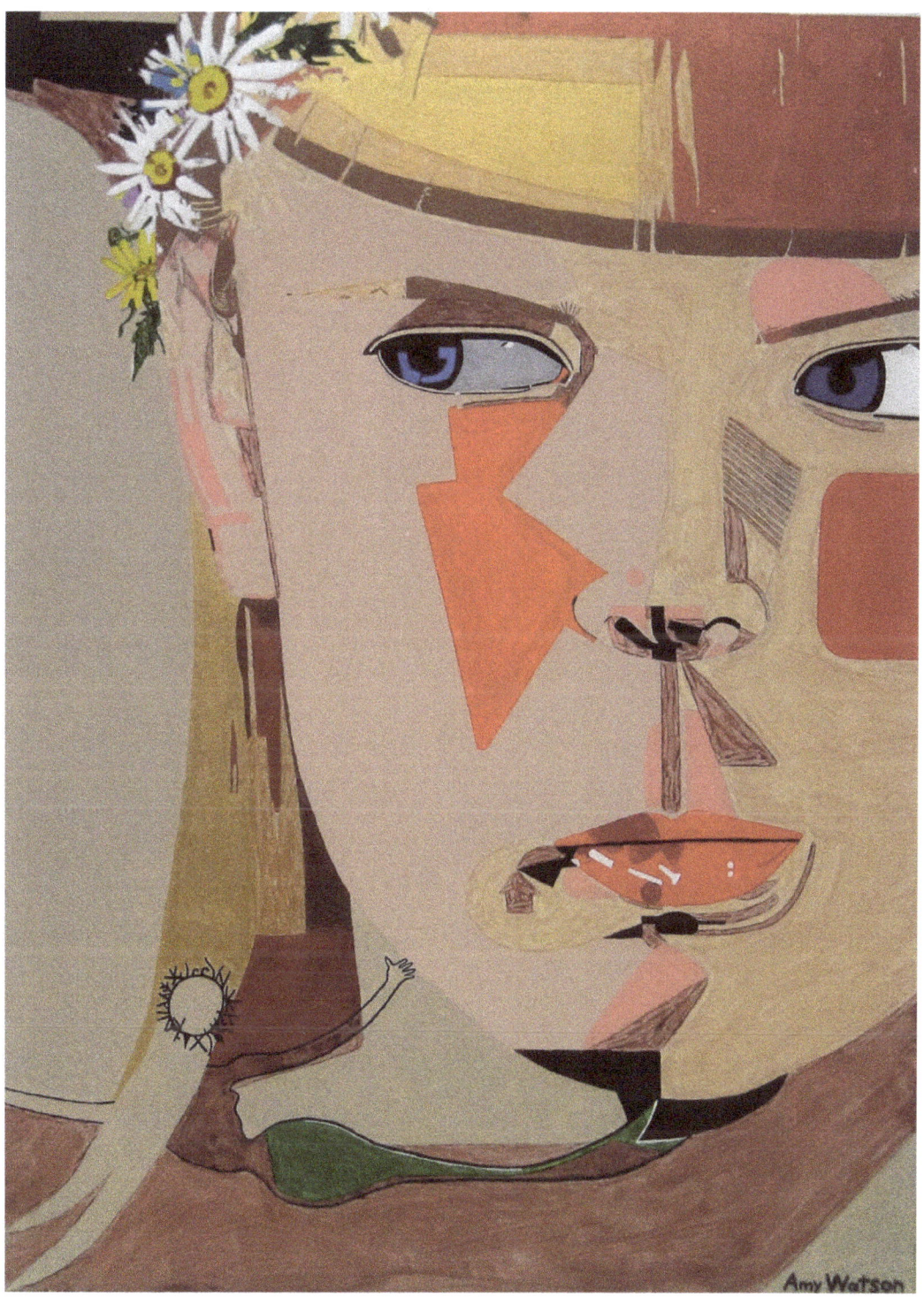

www.ingramcontent.com/pod-product-compliance
Lightning Source LLC
Chambersburg PA
CBHW041545220526
45473CB00014B/2963